Euro Error

By the same author:

POLITIQUE ÉCONOMIQUE : LE RAPPORT ROSA, Bonnel, 1983.

In collaboration:

L'ÉCONOMIQUE RETROUVÉE : VIEILLES CRITIQUES ET NOUVELLES ANALYSES, with Florin Aftalion *et alii*, Economica, 1978.

LA RÉPRESSION FINANCIÈRE, with Michel Dietsch, Bonnel, 1981.

THE WORLD CRISIS IN SOCIAL SECURITY, Bonnel, 1982.

THE ECONOMICS OF TRADE UNIONS : NEW ANALYSIS, Kluwer Nijhoff, 1983.

COMPARATIVE HEALTH SYSTEMS IN TEN INDUSTRIAL COUNTRIES, JAI Press, 1990.

Euro Error

Jean-Jacques Rosa

Translated under the direction of
Andrea Lyn Secara

1999
Algora Publishing

Algora Publishing, New York
© 1999 by Algora Publishing
All rights reserved. Published 1999
Printed in the United States of America
ISBN: 1-892941-00-7
Editors@algora.com

Originally published as *L'erreur européenne,* © Éditions Grasset & Fasqualle, 1998.

Library of Congress Cataloging-in-Publication Data 99-39176

Rosa, Jean Jacques.
    [L'erreur européenne, English]
    Euro error / Jean-Jacques Rosa ; translated from French under the direction of Andrea Lyn Secara.
    p. cm.
    Includes bibliographical references
    ISBN: 1-892941-00-7 (alk. paper)
    1. Monetary policy—European Union countries. 2. European currency unit. 3. Euro. I. Title.
HG925.R67 1999
332.4'94 dc21

The paper used in this publication meets the minimum requirements of the American National Standard for Information Sciences—Permanence of Paper for Printed Library Materials, ANSI $Z_{39.48-1992}$.

Algora Publishing wishes to express appreciation for the assistance given by the government of France through the Ministry of Culture in support of the preparation of this translation.

Table of Contents

Introduction

THE DILEMMA:
PROSPERITY OR THE SINGLE STATE,
A CHOICE MUST BE MADE

Who among Europeans could be anti-Europe? In the entire world, the Old continent is the place where the standard of living is the highest, where the culture is the oldest and, at the same time, the richest in diversity, where the way of life is most pleasant, and where democracy is the most widespread.

But if Europeans are so happy with their continent, what kind of Europe do they want for the future? Starting with the formation of the common market at the end of the Fifties, intended to restore the free exchange of goods, services, men and capital after the wave of protectionism and isolationism of the depression years and the war, the European leadership have gone on to erecting a plan for a monetary and thus a political Europe, that of a very great and a single State. Without that, they would have it, we would be relegated to decline and impotence and finally to obliteration. Not to want Europe unified, statist and monetarist, would be not to want Europe at all, as if the latter could admit only that one definition, only that one design; a typical example of politically correct thinking.

Actually, the European plan and consequently the future of the continent are marked by a deep ambiguity. The concept is economic and liberal when it comes to reintroducing free trade on a continent that had been given over to state intervention and protectionism for half a century: a single market and competition, in contrast to national statist intervention. Initially intended to support the United States against the Soviet threat, the European enterprise has retained a statist and military purpose, which tends to be defined as an end in itself.

It is this statist aspect that today comes into question precisely at the moment when the Soviet threat is disappearing, whereas the aspect of the market and competitive free trade has pretty much been carried out or is about to be completed. This is the moment that the European political leadership chooses to prod us down the path toward a single currency that leads logically and necessarily to the construction of a single federative or confederate State.

As long as Europe wants to preserve a political role in the world, that would appear to be a natural ambition. Of course, it does not please the Americans, who are afraid of competition in managing the planet's affairs. But that is all the more reason to do it! And it would be so much simpler for companies and travelers to use only one currency for the whole continent.

Unfortunately, this apparent simplicity is misleading. As scientists know, complex problems always have a solution that is clear, common sense, simple . . . and false! Upon superficial examination, the diversity that generates competition, the complexity of States and currencies as well as that of companies, always seems wasteful. To manufacture one product for every consumer, be it the black Ford Model T of the beginning of the century or the unisex uniform imposed on the Chinese by Mao, has a fatal allure for the social engineer slumbering inside each one of us.

In the same way, a single State seems as though it would be more efficient, more "rational" than several, to the Platonic and Cartesian minds that populate the hierarchical and administrative organizations.

That was the "solution" of Soviet planning invented by Lenin: to manage the country as one immense enterprise. We know how that turned out. The source of the error, as Hayek explained, is that central planning atrophies the production and diffusion of information that, by contrast, competition encourages. The single hierarchy dramatically reduces society's level of information and diminishes the quality of products as well as that of policies.

But what can we say, then, about the example of the United States? Do they not collectively prove the greater effectiveness of a great continental State able to create and multiply wealth at a rate never before achieved? Why not imitate them once again by creating the United States of Europe?

This parallel is tempting but false. Conditions at the end of the 20th century differ radically from those of the end of the 18th. When the American Federation was constituted, its population was homogeneous and very small. Creating the United States, in 1776, was rather like creating a country the size of Switzerland today. At the beginning of the 19th century, the Union hardly counted more than eight million inhabitants and it reached thirty million only on the eve of the War of Secession.

Thereafter, a small federal State was crowned with exceptional success; it became large because it was effective, it was not a State that was more effective because it was large from the outset. At the time, no one had in mind the creation of a giant by merging highly diverse nation-states. The United States represents the example of the small firm that succeeds, and thus grows, not that of the "national champion" imagined by civil servants who pride themselves in playing one of those construction games, like Lego's. So the American adventure was and will remain the exception.

Another fundamental difference should give the eurocrats pause. For a long time the Americans did not need a single currency. And they transitioned toward a central bank at the federal level over more than a century, from 1790 until the creation of the Federal Reserve System in 1913.

The idea of a single currency and a Very Great State belongs in the domain of administrative Utopia. First, because it proposes to create *ex nihilo* a common currency for several States, which has never succeeded in the past. Then, because it requires the construction of a single State, the continental Super-State, by merging great States of very different nature, and with heterogeneous populations, which has never been seen either.

The effort appears all the more absurd since the single currency will serve practically no useful purpose. On the contrary, it will necessarily harm the national economies. What is more, the Single State would be a fundamental aberration in the general development of private and public organizations. It will be expensive, useless, and will make still more difficult the essential reform of hypertrophied national States.

The elites in power in Europe actually propose to reproduce on this continent the model of ancient China, against the very spirit of the "European miracle" which led the nation-States of this small extension of Asia to dominate the world. How indeed did Europe come so far? Through competition and rivalry among the States, a process well described by British historian E.L. Jones[1]. It is the competition between rival nations that explains the unusual quality of the public services which the European populations enjoyed and which in turn determined the exceptional progress of the economy and the techniques characteristic of our continent, in modern times. This is the reverse of China, which very early on established a gigantic empire in which the State held a hierarchical monopoly on the production of low quality publicservices, which paralyzed innovation and destroyed the entrepreneurial spirit for several centuries. Tomorrow China will explode like the USSR and Yugoslavia. Europeans should avoid such a dead-end.

Hayek described the route toward servitude along which the victorious democracies were unwittingly advancing at the end of the Second World War. Today, we must avoid the dangerous slope of a decline that would affect Europe alone. The danger is no longer that of external totalitarianism, it is our own capacity for error and the soft totalitarianism of our elites.

Thus continental Europe is taking a wrong turn. The last decade of the 20th century will go down in history—for this club of old countries that count among the richest in the world—as a period of moral discouragement and economic decline.

Paradoxically, this period should have been marked by optimism and dynamism. The European nations succeeded in making a flawless economic comeback and achieved remarkable growth since the disaster of the Great Depression and the Second World War. In thirty years, between 1945 and 1975, they caught up with the standard of living and the technology of this century's world leader, the United States. With the disappearance of the communist threat on its eastern doorstep, and the opening on a world in full process of market globalization, Europe should enjoy a time of full optimism and daring changes. The reduction of the defense effort, the normalization of the price of energy, and the triumph of the democratic market system should have resulted in abundant peace dividends.

But quite to the contrary, we see moroseness and stagnation, an incapacity for reform, and aging of the structures that dominate since the collapse of the Soviet Union. Continental growth is stunted since the disinflation of the Eighties and the German reunification which was supposed, according to official speeches of the time, to bring an extraordinary dynamism to the economy beyond the Rhine as well as, by contagion, to those of all the other European partners. Instead, unemployment is now reaching levels close to those of the Thirties. The prospect of an indefinite pursuit of restrictive financial policies that choke expansion discourages those more enterprising who now choose to invest elsewhere.

Against this backdrop of deceleration and economic and social difficulties, the governments lack the courage to tackle fundamental reform of the welfare state—inordinately swollen since the last war by
the easy tax receipts that readily flow during exceptional growth.
Taxes and costs are reaching the limits of what the active population
can support, inflating the underground economy and contracting the
job market. Investors are turning away from a continent where the
cost of labor has become prohibitive compared to its productivity.
The productive basis of our societies is eroding, while the diminished
growth hinders the modernization of businesses.

Having been reformed in-depth, North America, Latin America
(having digested its debt crisis), Asia (the dragons, but also continental China, in spite of inevitable mishaps along the way), and Great
Britain all already feel the effects of a new world dynamism; but as a
result of their restrictive fiscal policies the majority of the continental
European economies are just limping along.

* *

However, this continental stagnation is not fatal. The European
economies have immense wealth. Their population still enjoys the
best education in the world. The social infrastructure is abundant and
well maintained. The political systems have long offered the advantages of advanced democracies.

And the formula for growth is no mystery. Countries that adopt
good macroeconomic policies, neither too lax nor too restrictive, and
especially those that can modulate them in a pragmatic way according
to the circumstances, those also that had the courage to launch basic
reforms of their welfare systems, of their taxation and regulations that
affect the real remuneration of labor, confirm the fact each day by
their superior performance. But they are almost all located outside of
Europe. The initiative is elsewhere now, in labor-dominated New
Zealand, in the dictatorial Chile, and then during their transition to
democracy, in the Eastern European countries who are living a revolu-

tion, in the literal sense, without precedent; in Great Britain and in the United States which showed the way to these structural reforms. But it is missing on our lagging continent, always one idea and one reform behind.

Growth, in a flourishing international environment, depends primarily on macroeconomic policy, i.e. of the State's financial policy. Indeed, macroeconomic policy is management of the currency (which is an instrument of national debt) and of the budget. Currency, omnipresent in the contemporary economy, is managed by governments and central banks; and through interest rates and the exchange rate it affects every decision made by producers and consumers. The budget that determines the aggregate spending depends on tax receipts and debt for its financing.

In some economies, the weight of the public sector in the broad sense, including the redistributive apparatus of the welfare state, now borders on half of the national income and takes in comparable amounts through taxation. Here, it is clear that the financial decisions of this weighty actor will affect the revenues and the financial decisions of all the other decision makers, whether corporations or households.

In France, the years 1986-1988 and 1994-1995 show that an expansive macroeconomic policy allowed the economy to show some life and to regain some of its dynamism, despite heavy regulation of the labor market. In the first period, only devaluation and the budget deficit made it possible to start up some activity again. In the second, deficit spending was the only source of a little growth, too modest because of the pursuit of a restrictive monetary policy. In both cases, structural reforms and improved flexibility were lacking, absent the strong expansion that could only have come with a much more realistic monetary policy.

Growth also depends on the structural reform of the State, and more particularly of the welfare state, which redistributes incomes and produces all types of subsidies, with the taxpayers' money. The growth of the welfare state, for a half-century, explains the current weight of the tax burden. This heavy apparatus, which initially played only an auxiliary role, has become enormous without reconsidering its objectives or its methods. It is characterized today by a staunch conservatism, with outdated and inefficiently centralized structures. Everywhere but on our continent, the State turns over to the private sector as much as possible of its production and protection activities, choosing to have others do, or to let them do, rather than doing things itself less effectively than competitive producers.

The State's expenditure is, in a way, the national economy's overhead cost. We are reaching the point where these overheads prove to be excessive and drag down businesses' potential to create wealth.

**

Which is to say, in the final analysis, that the responsibility for Europe's malaise falls on the policy that was chosen and the people who were responsible for implementing it. Contrary to the litany of governments that hide from any criticism behind the "tyranny of the financial markets" and the "constraints of globalization," supposed to deprive them of any room for maneuver, it should be clearly recognized that the financial policy of the State, the "macroeconomic" policy, is not dictated by the international environment. It results, in fact, from a choice that is basically political and not economic: that of the construction of a European State, intended to superimpose itself on the national states.

Instead of making it a priority to reform themselves, to restructure themselves by refocusing on their principal business as companies do, and seeking greater efficiency and therefore lower costs (that is, lower taxes), the European States have committed to a plan for external growth through political merger on a pan-European level. The Continent is no longer a simple area of free trade and cooperation among sovereign states. It has become, under the reign of the Socialists, a place for creating a super-State by merging the independent States that history had created, an undertaking that starts with the creation of a common currency. And this ambitious merger of the bodies politic is launched at the very moment when every country, all over the world, is tending rather to split and to divide in order to satisfy better their citizens' expectations, while saving on the overhead costs of managing large bureaucracies.

Admittedly, firms can seek to svae resources through merging, by distributing fixed costs over a greater sales base. But nothing of the sort is envisioned in connection with creating a European super-Stateth that will necessarily arise from the establishment of a single currency. On the contrary, everything points to the likelihood of superimposing an additional layer of political administration on top of those layers that are already in place in the national systems.

This venture, running counter to the realities of the end of the 20th century, constrains national governments to adopt an ultra-conservative financial policy that slows growth and induces an inexo-rable rise in the demand for public expenditure. Thus it proves self-destructive and compromises the very possibility of structural reform.

It is the same political view that diverts European governments from reforming the overgrown structures of the welfare state. This last, which constitutes a major department of the State enterprise, re-mains imperturbably immovable and refuses to adapt. It stays on, no matter what the cost—and it costs more and more in terms of lost em-ployment and growth, ever higher expenses, avoiding lay-offs and competitive restructuring whereas, confronting the same constraints, private firms and their employees adapt and bear all the cost of the necessary changes.

Justified until recent times by the exigencies of the Cold War, the attempt to build a European super-State via the creation of a single currency is no longer necessary. The world markets are mostly open, the Communist threat has disappeared and the Cold War with it.

It continues today only because it corresponds to the narrow interests and bolsters the ambitions of the French ruling class, whose first priority is to look after the electoral clientele of the civil servants and its centralizing culture. The programmatic construction of a new bureaucratic pyramid on the continental scale opens to our civil servant-politicians opportunities for career advancement and for power that are much more appealing than those of a national State that is subjected to competition and must reduce its operating expenses and its influence on the economy.

It corresponds also to the German leaders' desire for power (more than to the German voters, who are themselves not very keen on giving up the deutsche mark), and to their concern for regaining an international political role, which requires that France would go along. But the process remains quite as centralizing and statist as on this side of the Rhine: it strengthens the hand of the Reich. This expansionist policy was successful in the absorption of the Eastern Länder which, certainly, were naturally part of modern Germany as it was constituted just over one century ago. But it continues today with the single currency, repeating in a striking way the step that inaugurated the formation of the Empire in the 19th century, by integrating the southern States close to Prussia, and first by merging their currency with that of the North.

This conjunction of two statist traditions, the French and the German, misapprehending the current requirements and economic conditions, determines policies that are against the grain and whose fulcrum is the single currency. It is this political choice, in the tradition of a planned economy, contrary to the present economic needs, that explains euro-malaise and euro-stagnation.

The European impasse ultimately rests on several errors of judgment, incarnated in a series of prevarications which it is only too urgent to refute:

No, the single currency is not a decisive advantage for the continent. It is a drag.

No, the monetary squeeze and budgetary deflation are not imposed on us by the tyranny of the markets. And they do not prime the economy for healthier growth: on the contrary, they prevent it from finding its dynamic equilibrium and results from the political choice of the single currency as the instrument of the political merger.

No, finally, Europe does not need a super-State. It compromises our chances and stifles our economies by going against the requirements of the world economic and political environment. Everywhere, the time has come for reducing and diminishing the internal and external dimension of the States.

Choosing the single currency and the Very Great State is tantamount to giving up prosperity.

Chapter I

DEAD END

Continental Europe is in bad shape. Since the beginning of the decade, growth is weak, unemployment is up, investment has stagnated, and anxiety is taking hold. Among the countries of the continent France is particularly lagging with an unemployment record reaching toward thirteen percent of the working population, never seen since the Great Depression of the Thirties. And if inflation has disappeared, growth is feeble, far from the records of the post-war years!

What makes this situation particularly perverse is that it has established itself insidiously and persistently, in spite of interludes of remission—and without appearing catastrophic, which engenders individual fatalism and supports collective resignation. It does not incite anyone to react, either by a better analysis of the causes of this development, or by well-founded policies which could make an impact upon it.

WRONG WAY

Admittedly, many commentators decry the severity, economic but also social and political, of the incipient continental decline, the Euro-malaise. But one has the feeling, despite everything, that their cry of alarm is exaggerated. The economic difficulties are quite real but they remain nonetheless those of very rich countries where the standard of living has not declined. Growth has continued, even if it is weaker. All told, it is only a matter of a reduced rate of enrichment that would appear to require no response other than a little courage, patience, and a sense of future prospects.

The comparison, often made, with the Great Depression thus appears excessive. The economic situation of that time was characterized by plummeting production as well as a collapse of the general price level. It was an era of impoverishment and deflation. Unemployment was appreciably higher than today and it struck a population whose standard of living was much lower and who were only scantly compensated, if at all, for lost employment.

And all of the industrialized countries were involved, whereas until the Asian crisis, Europe was at a standstill, but in a global context of strong and even exceptional growth for some recently industrialized countries.

Governments and their advisers appear to us better armed, and incapable of making such gross economic policy errors as in the past. The dangers of deflation are now well-known and we must note, besides, that even though it is often announced as imminent, it does not occur in an obvious way anywhere. There has been no absolute and lasting drop in the general price level but a simple decline of the inflation rate that is bringing us gradually toward complete stability of prices. And, we are assured on all sides that zero inflation represents the ideal of good macroeconomic management—at least if one believes the managers of the most conservative central banks.

Should we then conclude that the concerns are ill-founded and that on the whole everything is fine, or that everything is going to be better? Unfortunately that is not the case. First, because allowing the economy to get bogged down is very costly, economically and socially, but especially because, far from being decreed by fate, it results from the most serious economic policy error made by the governments of the great democracies since the Thirties. It could have been avoided. It can be, still. Or else the malaise will persist, will be aggravated, and may well lead to an economic, social and political catastrophe.

It is the missed opportunity, current but also for the future, it is the continuation of dangerous and harmful policies that make the current economic and human waste intolerable.

THE RETURN OF MASS UNEMPLOYMENT

The degradation of the economic situation in Europe can be measured by the rise of mass unemployment linked to slower growth.

Having disappeared in the years of reconstruction and strong growth, it re-appeared at the end of the Sixties across the whole continent. Since then, it gradually settled in, growing by successive steps but without any unseemly outbursts, crossing threshold after threshold without causing the regularly heralded social explosion. It has, however, reached a magnitude that cannot be accepted.

The absence of a direct political reaction to this new unemployment should not deceive us. It does not mean that the phenomenon is negligible or that it does not entail a significant cost, individual and collective. This cost is simply more varied, diffuse, less immediately apparent and more difficult to measure in its multiple manifestations within rich societies than was the cost of the unemployment, in a context of poverty, in the Thirties.

If the situation of the unemployed had remained that of the inter-war years, today's unemployment would be politically insupportable. At the time, the one who lost his job was often the only financial support of his family. The standard of living was low. Compensation was limited and offered neither systematic protection in old age nor health insurance. Under such conditions, unemployment that strikes more than 10 percent of the working population must cause an intense social mobilization and instigate a speedy revision of economic policies.

We do not observe anything like that today because conditions have changed radically. Real incomes are much higher. The unemployed person's situation is less dramatic. There are usually several incomes per household. Unemployment compensation is good, and for fairly extended periods. Social coverage has been attained. The minimum living wage support (welfare), which is widely distributed, brings resources of substitution to those who do not manage to fit into the working world. Not working is no longer a radical impossibility for adults and teenagers. It no longer means the unbearable financial penalty of earlier days. Consequently, some people maintain that it is acceptable. One hears, particularly on the left, that well-compensated unemployment is better, after all, than poorly paid work. Better to be an unemployed person in Europe than a hamburger-flipper in the United States.

This thesis is caricatured in the recently popularized idea suggesting that our time might see the advent of the "end of work." Companies and markets would like that. This proposition suggests that there is no way to avoid it. The search for high productivity which international competition imposes on us will reduce the demand for low-skilled labor. We should look to a new era of leisure.

This vision, of course, is completely false, as the majority of economists stresses. It is not only misleading but also socially unacceptable.

It is one of the recurring topics of pseudo-economics, since the beginning of the Industrial Revolution, which attributes to technical progress increasing unemployment and the disappearance of work. After centuries of technical progress, it is obvious that this prophecy has never been fulfilled. Technical progress, as we know, causes a transitory unemployment quickly reabsorbed by the development of new activities generated by this same progress.

While it is true that the increase in the standard of living leads to a trend toward reducing the length of the working day, week and year, the reduction is modest. There is no direct relationship between the two and one should not confuse the latter with the abrupt shifts of activity and the sizable imbalances that characterize the fluctuations of the economic activity such as those that we currently observe. Moreover, the long termtrend toward reducing work time is requested by the employees themselves, whereas transitory mass unemployment is essentially endured as a loss of wealth. To seek to reduce the working time by a legislative decision, imposed by governments looking to erase the unhappy consequences of defective macroeconomic policies, is to confuse two completely distinct phenomena which are not of a comparable order of magnitude and do not respond to the same stimuli.

Actually, the low utilization of labor inherent in mass unemployment is explained by contingent economic conditions. All the studies show that the level of employment, in a given economy, varies in great proportion along economic cycles and is explained by a certain number of known parameters such as the price of labor, the level and growth of incomes, and global demand, which depend to a great extent on macroeconomic policies. Once again, the example of the United States during the last decades shows that unemployment hits highs and lows according to the economic situation, that it responds to incentives from the monetary and budgetary policy, and that consequently it is not fate that causes the regular increase in the number of the unsatisfied applicants for work.

One thus should not be resigned to, nor accept, the current European developments under the pretext that they arise from the modern mode of production and offer part of the population permanent leisure financed by those who work.

Mass unemployment is a social disaster, an economic absurdity that is not tenable in the long run.

A DIFFUSE DISASTER

The term disaster is certainly not too extreme nowadays when the least drought that compromises some harvests, the least flood that carries away a few houses, amply seem to justify its use.

Yet one rarely hears it used to describe the mass unemployment that more permanently impoverishes hundreds of thousands of people and ruins, directly and indirectly, thousands of lives each year.

It strikes hardest the least rich, and young people are much more severely affected than adults. The phenomenon is certainly not unusual and is, to some extent, normal insofar as young people are by definition in a trial period and seek their future path by experimenting, by groping their way into the labor market. It is the period of training and mobility.

Nevertheless, while the global rate exceeds 10 percent of the working population, unemployment among the 16-24 year olds reaches much higher levels, over 25 percent. That becomes a social phenomenon that largely exceeds the normal mobility of beginners and translates into difficulty for all, and finally the impossibility for many, to fit into the working world.

The consequences of these difficulties are dire. The young unemployed who are not able to get a foothold in a company lose their years for training. They do not accumulate professional experience and cannot acquire qualifications. Their chances of later fitting in are then reduced, decisively, as work experience often plays a more important part in income growth throughout the working life than does initial education, especially when that is limited.

The result is a major squandering of human potential for whole generations and which strikes, completely unjustly, those who are the least well trained to begin with and thus the least favored in a society that requires an increasing level of competence.

But it is much the same for all the other unemployed. It is the loss of immediate production that unemployment engenders that is usually emphasized. Compensated or not, the unemployed do not produce. One can measure the magnitude of this loss, at any given moment, by the difference between the production actually observed and that which would be obtained if the economy had continued its trend of full activity, which the economists call "potential" production. Everywhere in Europe, current production continues to stagnate, distinctly below its potential for growth. The waste is enormous.

But we do not measure the long-term consequences of unemployment for the unemployed themselves as we do for the community. Inactivity results in a loss of experience, for adults as well as for the young. Consequently, a real failure to gain competence is engendered by unemployment. And it becomes very significant in the event of long term unemployment. So much so that too long a stretch of unemployment becomes a heavy handicap when it comes to finding a job. Thus, for the individual unemployed person but also for the community, de-skilling or the reduced qualification that unemployment entails, i.e. the loss of human capital, reduces future productivity and production. The non-worker of today compromises the economic progress of tomorrow.

But the cost of unemployment is not only economic and concerns not only the unemployed. It turns up elsewhere, in the moral, social and political consequences of stagnation and under-employment.

The economic downturn is directly tied to social anxiety, to exclusion, to the recrudescence of delinquency and criminality. Nevermind the view of certain sociologists, that delinquency finds its source exclusively in the pathogenic characteristics of the environment, the individual having neither role nor responsibility. On the contrary, even when strictly applying the economists' yardstick, it is the individual who chooses both what he does and what he consumes. To launch out into criminal activity or delinquency results from an individual decision which rests on a comparison of the costs and the benefits.

The principle of this analysis, initially conceived by the Nobel laureate in Economics Gary Becker[1], is universal. It is easy to understand that the temptation to engage in illegal activity is stronger when it is impossible to find a normal job in the "official" economy and when, due to this fact, at the same time, one has few resources to sell. At the same time, the range of illicit possibilities is vast, from simply working "off the books," which implies tax evasion, to theft, selling drugs, and various violent crimes.

For any given constant level of social repression, the scarcer the normal employment opportunities, the higher the delinquency rate will be. Economic analysis thus agrees with the common sense view that the increasing agitation and delinquency in the "bad" neighborhoods, outside the causes generally cited such as the breakdown of the family and cultural distress, is ignited by the degradation of the economic conditions and the semi-permanent unemployment which strikes the least skilled young people, precisely those who for various reasons are concentrated in these areas.

Christian Bachmann and Nicole Guennec demonstrate this in a very precise analysis, which stresses the upsurge of both social unrest and delinquency since 1981, and especially since the beginning of the

Nineties[2]. Rioting is increasing in the "sensitive urban areas" and the "problem neighborhoods," whose number continues to rise, as does that of aggressive and violent incidents: 3,018 in 1992, 3,462 in 1993, 4,665 in 1994 and 6,818 in 1996 according to the *Renseignements généraux* [roughly equivalent to the FBI].

For young people without training, the prospects of finding a job and gaining skills are less. Their future in the world of official labor is doubtful. The alternative solution constituted by the choice of unofficial or illegal activities is all the more attractive, even irresistible. One thus observes a direct correlation between low wages and the criminality of the young. With age, wages increase and delinquency rates decrease; that of the 22-23 year olds is almost twice less than that of the 17-18 year olds[3].

But for young people without jobs the wage level is meaningless, anyway. And when this situation is prolonged, the probability of participation in illicit activities increases.

Seeking to solve this problem through repression, by increasing the resources of ministry of justice and the police force, can and must form part of an overall law and order strategy. However, they cannot suffice in themselves. It is not the most efficient method for the community as a whole, since stabilizing the level of delinquency would require constantly increasing the resources devoted to repression as the unemployment of the young people will continue to increase. One might also consider social and educational action in managing families, or try to transform people's culture and mindset. But these are methods whose effectiveness remains limited and which require at the same time much perseverance and considerable human and, consequently, financial resources.

The most direct policy and the most immediately effective in reducing this social waste consists of stimulating employment and reducing unemployment among young people. That requires specific economic policies, to which we will return.

Meanwhile, the economic sources of delinquency and disorder lead to another social consequence about which there is also much speculation. Unemployment and exclusion from the official labor market determine a rapid decomposition of the fundamental social ethic, the ethic of labor, which structures behaviors.

Collective depression, the asocial behaviors of depredation, of vandalism, of gratuitous aggression, develop in parallel to "weakness" in the economy. This, which is different from traditional poverty or misery, comes from the absence of personal prospects, of the loss of hope, and marginalization from official society. The marginalization is felt all the more when economic degradation is only relative, so that the prosperity of some is seen side by side with, and highlights the distress of the others. And this distress, which is no longer glaring, does not particularly attract either compassion or altruism since it is not quantified directly in material terms such as hunger or the impossibility of clothing oneself. Exclusion, when it is immaterial and moral, is only the more insidious and destructive.

A measurable trace of this can be observed in the development of pessimism in Europe. Opinion polls reveal a drop in the morale of Europeans in step with the declining growth and rising unemployment. A short trip on the *Eurostar* (the high speed train linking the UK to France) shows the astonishing difference in atmosphere between London, where intense activity, feverish imagination, dynamism and optimism dominate—and the continent, which appears suddenly dull and stagnant by comparison.

The statistics on youth suicide, which is increasing chronically, should hold our attention. There again, without claiming to explain everything, the economists show that the fluctuations of the suicide rate are directly linked to the prospect for individual activity and enrichment. All things being equal, there are more suicides during a period of recession and unemployment. That suicide is increasing among young people more rapidly than among adults is, furthermore, consistent with the unequal decline of the prospects from one group to another. It is the young people who suffer more from the poor performance of the European economy, at the moment when they must build their professional future and when there are fewer and fewer of them to pay for the retirement of the old, whose number is increasing.

Lastly, the rise of xenophobia in France and Germany, for example, is a particularly worrisome consequence of the loss of jobs and the declining growth. It now constitutes a political risk that cannot be overlooked. This political backsliding, traditional in difficult times, is explicitly tied to growing unemployment, as the foreigner is accused of stealing jobs from the nationals. Let us not forget that a similar phenomenon developed in Great Britain at the time of economic stagnation under the impetus of Enoch Powell, and in the United States in the years of uncertainty, when Governor Wallace and other politicians of the extreme right mobilized a considerable fraction of the votes. All this undercurrent was rendered inconsequential by the return of prosperity. This shows that moralizing speeches on their own have little chance of reversing the trend toward political extremism if the economy continues to drag, thereby destroying jobs.

But the social disaster is not limited to these effects, serious as they are. Unemployment also reduces the ratio of the effectively employed within the working population, which includes the employed and the unemployed. According to the official definition, the "unemployed" are people of working age who would like a job at current wages but do not find any. When their number increases, the global activity ratio decreases. This development is a challenge to common sense, whereas the demographic trend is already alarming from the standpoint of financing the systems of transfers and redistribution that take such an important role in the continent's economies.

Reduced growth and mass unemployment thus call into question the equilibrium that was based on a higher rate of economic progress. There follows a series of chronic problems that are difficult to solve:

lower tax revenues, increase in the social transfer costs, public deficits, difficulties in financing retirement systems and health insurance. These transfers, financed by the tax on labor, are going up at a rate that has become unsustainable, causing a heavier burden on the economy and increased unemployment.

It is impossible to go on in this way, especially given the problem of retirement which requires a growing working population to finance the increasing numbers of pensions, which must be paid over longer and longer periods of retirement. The demographic deadlines, which will be felt heavily in 2005, must be addressed starting today.

Having a reduced working population while maintaining unchanged public expenditures will increase the tax burden per worker. In a perverse way, the non-worker is thus treated better than the worker: the productive workers are crushed and discouraged by the increasing pressure of the payroll taxes, at the same time, the growth of the underground or unofficial economy is encouraged, which, in turn, dries up the financial resources of the States and increases the tax burden on the "official" working population.

Transfers in kind, which are not subject to tax, are then in greater demand than monetary incomes, which take the full brunt of all the social taxes. We are increasingly moving toward an economy of redistribution to the detriment of the economy of production. Increasingly heavy transfers rely on a productive activity that is being reduced. The Tax State is heading toward hypertrophy.

Here again the tendency cannot continue indefinitely, because more intense international competition translates rising national tax burdens into the relocation of businesses and the rapid loss of economic substance. Tax competition between countries to attract investments and businesses diverts resources from the countries whose tax costs are highest. This is why economic slowdown, which reduces the utilization of the productive potential, will intensify the Tax State's pressure on the economy and bring the country which is its victim to be excluded gradually from international competition.

Thus the future is limned in a much darker tone than the simple report of the current downturn would have us think. After the demographic shocks of 2005 and 2015, the impoverishment of retirees and declining prospects for low-skilled young people are likely to combine in a dangerously explosive mixture.

That is why it is so important to make the right diagnosis. An accurate statement of the problem is essential to the definition and the implementation of appropriate policies — which must not be further delayed. The need is just as urgent as in the Thirties, even if the circumstances appear different.

But, for that, we must give up political taboos and put an end to the conspiracy of silence that binds and dominates the political and economic leaders of our countries.

CAUSES THAT ARE KNOWN, BUT NOT ACKNOWLEDGED

The political neglect of the economic and social problems raised by wide-scale unemployment is explained in the same way as the difficulty of analyzing and measuring its diffuse effects. A faulty economic policy is preached as well by the political left as by the right, and by the managers of the welfare State, appointed jointly by the employers' unions, the trade unions and the government. There is, in short, a corporatist collusion to defend a system and policies that maintain and increase unemployment. The unemployed, for their part, compensated in various ways, are to some extent reduced to silence by their position as aid recipients, which enables them to obtain community assistance without quid pro quo. In addition, since young people are often not integrated into the social, political and trade-union life, they are poorly represented politically. They are "outsiders" who

weigh little vis-a-vis the "insiders," organized groups and political organizations. Thus debate about unemployment is avoided.

However, as all the economists and corporate leaders know but no
politician wants to hear—unemployment could be reduced considerably and in a rather short timespan, if its principal causes, which are
well identified, were attacked seriously. But nothing is done nor was
it ever done in this sense, counter to the affirmations of practically all
the political leaders who breezily adopt François Mitterrand's cele-
brated prevarication, "We have tried everything we could to fight unemployment."

What was done actually amounts to a permanent feud over various
administrative gadgets and the distribution of various forms of assistance, the "social approach to unemployment," and to half-hearted initiatives about job-sharing. Job-sharing was a pseudo-solution resulting
from an administrative vision of the economy as a fixed number of
budgetary "positions" to distribute among too many applicants. Each
of these attempts was more ineffective than the last. This is even
starting to be recognized, so that some people are advocating plans to
cut the considerable amounts of public funds devoted to activities
which serve no useful purpose or, worse still, contribute to increasing
the total volume of unemployment because of the perverse incentives
that they generate.

What every economist knows and says, in vain, is that one could
be optimistic again if good policies were adopted, because the total
volume of employment is elastic. It can increase considerably with
economic growth, but also as a function of the cost of labor which includes both the level of wages and the cost of the regulations and the
taxation that hit employment.

The development of unemployment depends on macroeconomic
policy, monetary and budgetary, on tax policy, and the regulations
that contribute to increasing the cost of labor and weakening the demand for it in favor of capital requirements.

Financial Conservatism and Macroeconomic Repression

The primary factor in unemployment is macroeconomic policy, which can, in the short run (say, eight to eighteen months), inflate or depress the business and household demand for goods and services. When it is restrictive, and leans too much in the direction of financial conservatism, as in our case since the beginning of the Nineties, it slows down the growth of credit and of aggregate demand by reducing activity and by depressing employment. The responsibility for that hinges on the unfortunate choice of aligning the franc and the mark. The choice of a fixed exchange rate has led the French monetary authorities to permanently maintain the short term interest rates at a level higher than the economic situation justifies, in order to attract international capital to France and to thus support a parity of the franc which does not correspond to its level of spontaneous equilibrium.

Certainly they tell us that the short-term interest rates, fixed by the Bank of France, have dropped considerably since the beginning of the decade. But that is explained mainly by the spectacular drop of inflation, which is not unique to our country but happened in all the developed countries. What actually counts for borrowers, whether households or companies, is not the "nominal" interest rate, slightly over 3 percent today, but the "real" interest rate, corrected for inflation. The correctly measured inflation, which is lower than that of the official index, probably does not exceed 0.5 percent, which gives real short term interest rates of 2.5 percent or more, much higher than the historical standard which has been, on average, almost nil.

Countries that jump-started their economies at the beginning of the decade, like the United States, brought their nominal short term rates to practically zero. But our monetary policy remains restrictive, adding the effect of high real rates that dissuade consumers and investors to the overvaluation of the exchange rate in the wake of the mark, which discourages exporters.

On the whole, economic activity is constantly suppressed, for the sole benefit of the good reputation of our financial authorities when they want to sell government bonds to international investors. But added to this deflationary influence of the exchange and the interest rates is the effort to reduce the budget deficits, imposed by the Treaty of Maastricht according to arbitrary and economically unfounded standards. The effort to balance public finances is carried out, in France, not through spending cuts but by increasing the tax burden—which reduces global demand still further, as any CEO would know.

Where better managed countries are seeing vigorous and sustained growth, like the United States, Great Britain and Italy (until the recent period of revaluation of the lira to qualify for membership in the Euro club), the countries of financial conservatism, blind like France, are lagging and achieve only weak growth, in spite of the absurdly inflated forecasts of the official authorities and economists.

The low average growth rate we have been experiencing since 1990 does not make it possible to stop the rise of unemployment. By contrast, the periods of stronger growth such as 1986-1988 under the Chirac government, or even the slight recovery of 1994-1995 due to the Balladur government's budget deficit policy, had allowed things to improve a little.

But political taboo forbids the political leaders from openly admitting this simple reality and adopting a less conservative macroeconomic policy, which is essential. This taboo is called "single currency." In the absence of any inflationary pressure in France and in the world, and with the national debt not reaching an alarming level in our country, it is the desire to maintain a fixed parity with the Deutsche mark, and respect for the arbitrary criteria of Maastricht which lead our government to apply to the French economy a self-defeating financial purging that paralyses economic activity.

We must give up this policy which is responsible, according to experts, for at least 4 and perhaps 5 of the 12.5 and more percentage points of unemployment recorded today. And the effects of a new macroeconomic policy of floating exchange rates, short term interest rates brought down to zero and reduction of the overall tax burden could be felt in the space of a few months.

The Antisocial Effects of the Tax On Labor

The second cause of unemployment is the particularly high, and quickly growing, level of the tax on labor represented by social security contributions. The tax on gasoline discourages petrol consumption; the tax on alcohol reduces liquor consumption; the payroll tax decreases the demand for labor that emanates from businesses, thus boosting unemployment.

Some still believe that the social security contributions constitute an "advantage" for employees because the employers would actually bear the burden of the tax. But that is not what happens, as shown by economic studies and in particular those of the OECD[4]. It is the employees who bear the brunt of the real charge since take-home pay drops, on the labor market, more or less in proportion to the increase of social security taxes. However, the employers do support, despite everything being said to the contrary, part of the charge, in the form of an increase in the total cost of labor (the gross salary plus contributions of the employers and employees) when the rate of the tax increases. This increase in the cost of labor dissuades them from creating jobs. It becomes more advantageous for them to try to automate operations and reduce their workforce. But at the same time the total volume of investment hardly increases, as long as global demand, governed by the monetary and budgetary policy, remains stagnant.

The taboo, for this second cause of unemployment, is again political. To reduce the payroll tax would require giving households the responsibility for directly purchasing health insurance from public and private insurers. This could be a legal obligation as is the case for auto insurance. That would take the place of the employer's withholding the amount of the tax that is immediately transferred to the monopolist insurer, social security. It is possible thus to introduce competition into the health insurance sector and reduce social security contributions while maintaining the redistributive role of social security. The payroll tax would no longer include an insurance premium but would be only a solidarity tax, much lighter than the current contributions, from the higher-paid employees to help the least-favored employees to buy health coverage equivalent to that which they have today, but at lower cost. This reform would not be antisocial, contrary to the claims of those advocates of the monopoly system, who are pleased to maintain the confusion between insurance, monopoly, and redistribution of incomes, in order to frighten the public and to prevent any reform.

But no politician wants to clarify the discussion and question the current health insurance monopoly, generator of revenues that the social security lobby eagerly defends, supported in this conservative combat by the employers' federations and by the employees who manage it. The change would require a considerable public information effort, and an opening of the debate—from which we are still very distant.

Regulations that Exclude

The third factor of unemployment also rests on a particularly resistant taboo: the regulations that increase the cost of labor, and minimum wage legislation above all. It has been proven abundantly, in every country in the world, that legal minimum wages destroy jobs for young and low-skilled workers[5].

It is said today that legislated minimum wages no longer have any harmful effects because of the existence of the RMI [*Revenue mini-*

mum d'insertion, a form of welfare payment], which dissuades its recipients from actively seeking a job at wages that are close to the
minimum. But this conclusion is exaggerated. Indeed, the RMI is
appreciably lower than minimum wages, and young people who want
to get into the workforce and advance later cannot regard it as a long
term solution. They would benefit from a lowering of the minimum
wages that would largely open the doors to first jobs. In addition, the
SMIC [*Salaire minimum interprofessionel de croissance*, a guaranteed
minimum wage tied to an index] constitutes a "floor" to which the social security contributions are added. As a result, the minimal cost of
labor for the firm is well above the SMIC, and has reached a level
such as to discourage many employers from hiring first-time or low-
skilled employees whose productivity is lower than that cost.

There, too, the taboo is political. Against all the evidence, the responsible elected officials want to believe that the SMIC has no harmful effects on the employment of unskilled young people. In reality,
interest in the minimum wage, which explain the taboo, comes from
the fact that it guarantees the employees who are already in place in
the companies against competition from young people trying to get in.
The insiders thus take advantage of the outsiders, who are condemned
to wander on the outskirts of the world of employment and training.

In a normally sustained economic situation, simple abolition of the
SMIC could create a few hundred thousand jobs for the most underprivileged young people. But what political leaders will take risks to
defend these unorganized clients?

To say that there exists in France a "preference for unemployment"
is both provocative and inaccurate. The expression indeed makes one
believe a choice was made, resulting from a social consensus. It is
nothing of the sort. It is the political leaders and the protagonists of
the corporate game who forbid the establishment of effective policies
to alleviate unemployment while enforcing the law of silence as to the

three taboos which stand in the way of open and public discussion of these policies.

If these taboos could be broken, adequate policies would be tested immediately and unemployment could quickly diminish. But for that, one would need an enlightened and open democratic debate. And that would start by clearly putting up for social reflection, first and foremost, the close connection between growth and unemployment. Whatever may be the various causes of unemployment, their effects vary according to the growth rate. A strongly expanding economy attenuates them; a recession or a simple slowdown of growth aggravates them.

Unemployment is Not Inevitable

To be convinced, one needs only examine the contrasted developments of unemployment in the United States and in the European Union.

Unemployment follows a specific trajectory in Europe. It increases in stages, but apparently irreversibly. The contrast is striking with the United States, where it fluctuates fairly regularly according to the economic conditions, growing during economic downturns and shrinking again in expansionary phases. But, on the whole, it when it shrinks, it tends to gravitate toward its low in the Sixties. That is particularly true of the expansion now in progress, exceptionally strong and long lasting, which brings it to about 5 percent or less of the working population without, for all that, the manifestation of any notable inflationary tendencies.

The American course soundly proves an important fact. Contemporary mass unemployment is not decreed by fate. It can be cut back to its irreducible, "frictional," "structural" or "natural" minimum (all these terms are interchangeable) by vigorous expansion.

And whatever may be the influences which contribute to increasing structural unemployment, there is a solid link between the growth of production and the alleviation of unemployment. This is what the macroeconomists call the "Okun's Law," named for the former Chairman of the White House "Council of Economic Advisors," who was first to analyze this empirical regularity. In France, one can observe as an approximation that below 3.5 to 4 percent growth of production, it is nearly impossible to reduce the rate of unemployment.

Comparing the American and European unemployment curves clearly emphasizes the recent divergence on the two sides of the Atlantic. The gap widens starting at the beginning of the Eighties. Whereas the United States records a spectacular fall, European unemployment is distinguished by two strong surges, from 1979 to 1985, then again since 1991.

Thus we must conclude that it is not simply "natural," due to the rigidities of the labor market or to the conditions of international competition, phenomena which, being structural, hardly change from one year to another. It must depend on factors that develop and change quickly, in other words on the business conditions.

And an examination of European growth statistics confirms it. The two periods of strong up-ticks in unemployment are also periods of declining growth, the beginning of the Eighties on the one hand and the Nineties on the other. Conversely, the end of the Eighties, which was characterized by a renewed expansion of the European economies, partly under the influence of the oil counter-shock (the marked drop in the price of oil and raw materials), corresponds to a very clear reduction in the unemployment rate. Proof again that unemployment is not decreed by fate.

But things get more interesting still, if one continues the analysis. The two phases of upsurge in unemployment and lower growth in Europe are not unexplained. They stem from deliberated macroeconomic policies. The first corresponds to the fight against double-digit inflation at the end of the Seventies, inflation which arose itself from massive increases in the price of oil, in 1973 and in 1979. All the

European governments of the time established restrictive monetary and budgetary policies: increasing the interest rates through intervention by the central banks, reducing budget deficits by raising taxes. There followed almost immediately a very marked braking of economic activity, under the influence of which inflation then gradually slowed down. The fight against inflation thus bore its fruit, at the price of a recession, just as it did in America a little before, in 1979-1981, at the time of the "Volcker Recession" (the name of the Chairman of the Federal Reserve System, who set up a particularly vigorous policy of monetary cooling).

The second outbreak of European unemployment then came into play after too short a period, during which it had regressed slightly. The economic slowdown at the beginning of the Nineties reversed this new trend and led to a return to higher levels of unemployment.

This time the economic slowdown resulted from different circumstances. German reunification caused, in that country, a massive increase in public spending towards the Länder of the East. That generated inflationary tendencies, which the Bundesbank undertook to fight vigorously with a very restrictive monetary policy. And the effect of that was to stop inflation and, at the same time, growth.

But the other European countries had just confirmed and tightened the fixing of their exchange rates with Germany. To maintain these parities they were then obliged to set short term interest rates (controlled by the central banks) at the same level as German rates. Otherwise capital would have migrated toward Germany, which would have been more remunerative, and the exchange rates would have had to be revised.

These restrictive monetary policies, adopted in several countries in order to go along with the German policy and to maintain fixed exchange rates, halted expansion everywhere in Europe. It especially affected those countries, France in particular, where there was no more inflationary trend. Such policies did not correspond to the needs of the moment, and their recessive impact was devastating for growth. Unemployment was propelled toward new heights.

LOOKING FOR LOST GROWTH

The progressive foundering of European growth in this *fin de siècle* is indisputable. It is not debatable, despite the official and quasi-official economic forecasts, that is, those of the practically every economist in the region, who announce to us with delightful regularity that prosperity is just around the corner. The optimistic bias of these forecasts needs no further proof. They are indeed always higher than the effective growth rates later recorded, whereas the recognized difficulty of forecasting and the errors which must inevitably creep in should, if the exercise were carried out objectively or impartially, lead to errors that would be distributed about as often on the side of under-estimation as that of over-estimation. It seems that the pressure of the monetary and governmental authorities is strongly felt by the economists who are too circumspect to give the opinion that the king has no clothes and that the difficult periods are far from over.

However, to note the disappointing performance of the European economy and that its phases coincide with outbreaks of unemployment is not sufficient grounds for concluding that macroeconomic policies are entirely responsible for the plague. After all, the slack growth could stem from other public policies, for example those relating to income transfers, or regulations, or the tax structure, or it could just as easily be simply the result of factors beyond the will and the capacity of the national governments to take action, like the maturing of our economies or increased competition from the emerging countries.

Thus we must try to determine more rigorously the causes of the downturn, in order to define the suitable remedies.

This question clearly was the object of sustained interest among economists during the period of 1975-1985, and then again at the beginning of the Nineties, that is, during the two periods of decline. The explanations suggested fall into three main categories.

The first refer to natural and unavoidable factors: the end of a period of correction of an earlier lag in the economy and the increased cost of technical progress since the end of the Seventies.

Others advance a "traditional" diagnosis re-christened "Eurosclerosis." The deceleration would be explained by the growing costs of labor, due to the taxes that finance an invasive welfare state and due to the many regulations that rigidify the labor market and prop up wages. Increased competition from newly industrialized countries where the wages are very low would, by comparison, make the cost of European labor even more prohibitive.

Others, finally, suggest a macroeconomic or "Keynesian" diagnosis but which one might just as easily describe as "monetarist," with respect to demand at the enterprise level. It is the insufficiency of global demand, resulting from overly restrictive monetary and budgetary policies, which chokes growth and causes rising cyclical unemployment.

The choice of the diagnosis, generally, is not made dispassionately, according to scientific considerations alone. According to his political preferences, each one will rather lay the emphasis on such and such cause. Firms would emphasize the cost of labor related to the welfare state and on the loss of international competitiveness vis-a-vis newly industrialized countries. The trade unions and the Left exonerate the welfare state and income transfers from any responsibility but, like the owners, they denounce the globalization of markets and competition from the low wage countries as well as the tyranny of the financial markets which require companies to show ever-increasing profits. The central governments and bankers also deplore the hard times resulting from competition from low wage countries with rudimentary or non-existent social policies, but they use that as an argument to defend the conservative monetary and financial policies which they prefer.

The economists close to these different milieux also tend to prefer such and such explanation for reasons more political than scientific, which explains the poverty and the confined atmosphere of the intellectual debate as to which economic policies it would be advisable to adopt.

It is, however, possible to arrive at an overall diagnostic, more rigorous and more complete, starting from the partial explanations—some of which are complementary more than contrary. Let us briefly examine the range of these various analyses and their possible compatibility.

Economic Maturity?

This hypothesis was already formulated in the Thirties to explain the Great Depression. Today as then, the slowdown would come from an insufficiency of investment, the principal force that drives growth, there being fewer opportunities to invest profitably in a mature economy.

Nowadays the thesis is presented a little differently. Europe's slowdown would be only the other side of the coin of three decades of exceptional growth due to the rebuilding of economies devastated by the Second World War and to a catchup of the lost growth of the Thirties and Forties. Since 1973, the European economies have returned to their secular growth trend, a little higher than two percent per year if one is to take into account the experience of the 19th century.

It is in fact very probable that part of the slowing of growth corresponds to a simple return to normal after the acceleration of "the glorious thirty," between 1945 and 1975. It is, certainly, easier to grow rich by imitating the technical progress accumulated elsewhere than by creating new products and new manufacturing methods. Standing behind the United States, a follower in terms of standard of living as well as innovation and technical progress throughout the century, the European economies caught up with the per capita output of America toward the middle of the Seventies. From now on, they must innovate by themselves to grow, which is more difficult and more expensive than to rely on imitation or adaptation.

At the same time, the international opening of trade and the sometimes dazzling debut of newly industrialized countries have brought unexpected and tougher competitors against the European firms. The conditions in which they had prospered thus changed radically in the space of a few years.

This analysis is not precisely new since I presented it fifteen years ago[6]. After the war there was a true European "golden age" while we made up for the lost growth during the pre-war years and the world crisis. Since then, many theoretical and empirical works have confirmed this interpretation[7]. The development of seventeen European countries from the beginning of the century until the Nineties shows that the recent growth is in line with the age-old trend extrapolated from the years prior to the First World War. Production, which had fallen below this century-long trend in the Thirties and Forties, got back on track between 1945 and the middle of the 1970s. On this date the gap of production per capita between the United States and all the countries of Europe (except Great Britain) was reduced for the first to time a level lower than in 1913. At the end of the Seventies the economic recovery was complete.

This recovery was essentially due to massive investment in new equipment incorporating the most recent technology. That explains a second aspect of the deceleration posterior to 1973, the cost of technical progress suddenly rising for the European economies.

The technological catching-up was particularly fast until the middle of the Seventies, and played an important part in bringing closer together the per capita production figures for industrialized countries. But this phenomenon was essentially exhausted in the Eighties, which leaves no room for future growth, unless there is an autonomous investment effort to create further technical progress[8].

Europe is now in the same position as the United States: it must create for itself the conditions of its own prosperity. But this thesis, which explains part of the observed decline, is not sufficient to account either for the economic fluctuations of growth in the Eighties, nor for the distinct pulling back in the Nineties, which places Europe far behind the United States. Indeed, the latter, imitated more recently by Great Britain, has shown that fate alone does not predetermine slow growth and unemployment for mature economies.

In addition, the simple inflecting of the growth trend after 1973 does not in itself explain the rise of unemployment fifteen years later. This response time appears excessively long, even for labor markets struck by institutional sclerosis. Moreover, there is no reason for growth that is lastingly slower to be accompanied by higher unemployment (after a period of adaptation during which those who go out into the labor market must get used to asking for only the smallest increases in wages, in proportion with the smaller growth in the productivity of labor). One can imagine that, for a while, the demand for wage increases might continue in accordance with old practices and be too high for the more modest progress of productivity that now obtains. But the adjustments take place eventually. Then there can be full employment, whatever the long term rate of growth.

Furthermore, the new growth trend should not change appreciably from one year to another. Thus it cannot explain the short term variations of the economic situation, of activity and unemployment. And it can hardly explain the divergent developments between Great Britain and Italy and other countries on the continent.

Lastly, the European economies as a whole did worse still than their historical trend in recent times, limiting growth to 1.5 percent on average whereas the long term trend is higher than 2 percent.

The Traditional Diagnosis: The Cost of Labor and
Eurosclerosis

This is the explanation preferred by business people, resulting from
their daily management challenges, but also that of conservative financiers who would exonerate the exchange rate and interest rate policies
from any responsibility.

This analysis makes the weakening of the growth depend on the
rise of a permanent "structural" unemployment, which results from
excessive regulation of the labor market and the hypertrophy of the
social protection systems.

For a company, output and employment depend on the cost of production, whose principal component consists of the remuneration of
labor. When its cost is too high compared to its productivity, employment must be reduced, either by substituting machines, less expensive
than labor, or by restricting the volume of production.

For the economy as a whole, the mechanism works the same way.
Thus the source of Europe's declining growth between 1975 and 1985
was attributed, a few years ago, to "Eurosclerosis," a term coined by
Herbert Giersch, the former President of the Institute of World Economy Institute in Kiel, to indicate a cost of labor that was too high and
that could not adapt to a decline. Thus, the "sclerotic" labor market
reduced companies' output and consequently economic growth.

Wage Rigidity

According to the Eurosclerosis theory, the reason wages are so resistant to reduction—their insufficient "flexibility," to use a current
euphemism—may be found in the multiplication of the interventions
of the welfare state and particularly in the development of regulations
on hiring and firing, but also in minimum wage regulations and the

generous unemployment compensation, all of which limit the mobility of labor. A subsidized employee, whose employment is protected by a tangle of legalities, will avoid mobility and will not have to accept possible income reductions, even if labor productivity decreases.

The result is a high cost of labor, higher than its level of equilibrium. It follows that new job creation will be rare and that the victims of this situation are those who seek to enter the labor market for the first time, in particular those who have only poor skills, and whose productivity is insufficient to make profitable the relatively high wages in force on the market.

In addition, if work applicants, usually covered by unemployment insurance (and generously, in France—compared to the rest of Europe, except Germany)—are in a hurry to find an employer, the employers seek, for their part, to replace labor with machines, which reduces global employment. This temptation is all the stronger since retirement and health insurance are financed by the tax on wages, which further increases the labor cost for companies.

Finally, subsidies poured in through the framework of industrial policy provide life support to the least profitable firms and bolster existing jobs, also contributing to wages' resistance to any downward adjustment.

State interventions on the labor market, the social protection system in the broad sense, have the effect of increasing the cost of labor for companies, therefore reducing employment and consequently production, which clearly shows the parallel between the growth of social security spending, generating increases in the tax on labor, and the mean level of unemployment[9].

This diagnosis can be described as "traditional" because it represented the dominant train of thought explaining unemployment and the Depression, before Keynes and the development of macroeconomic analysis. It is, in particular, that of Jacques Rueff in France in the Thirties. According to this analysis, the severity of unemployment and the Depression resulted from an excessive cost of labor that was maintained in spite of unemployment, on a market distorted by legal interference, indemnification, and pressure from trade unions.

This analysis is incontrovertibly relevant as well for the Eighties and the recent years of Euro-malaise (1990-1997). In particular, the heavy tax on labor that the social security taxes represent explains the development of structural unemployment in Europe. The absence of downward flexibility of wages also accounts for the contrast observed between the American growth model, rich in employment, and the European model that maintains wages but barely creates jobs, as Paul Krugman emphasizes[10]. However, less employment, if machines are not substituted for labor, also means less production and less growth.

The debate about Europe's non-performance is split along the most visible difference with the United States, which is the presence of a vast welfare state in Europe whereas its role in more circumscribed on the other side of the Atlantic.

Whence the exhortation for "structural" reform, for the social systems, and for growth in the flexibility of the labor market, the diagnostic maintained by the OECD in the 1980s as well as by the liberal economists in general, but also by the monetary authorities and the European governments. The examples of the United States and Great Britain are often cited. Their strong growth and the speedy reduction of unemployment experienced in the Nineties would reward the courageous reforms of the State and the liberalization of the labor market.

The thesis even goes a little further for those who hold with supply-side economics. According to them, it is not only the social security tax that reduce the employment potential of firms; it is all of the taxes that penalize economic activity. They add up to a production cost that must be born by both households and companies. Reducing tax rates, and more especially the marginal rates which are higher than the average rates when the tax is progressive, should have the effect of strongly stimulating growth.

In that case, it is not the welfare state that should be reformed, but all public spending, which should be reduced in order to spur production.

This explanation, however, runs into several difficulties. Although the negative effect of taxation on any activity is undeniable and is well established, in theory as well as in practice, the empirical data intended to measure the overall impact of taxation on growth are not conclusive. The results are contradictory from one study to another, and the extent of the phenomenon is considered to be major in some instances but generally minor, even insignificant.

There are several reasons for that. On the one hand general taxation, which feeds the State budget, strictly speaking, has hardly gone up in the industrialized countries in the past several years (if one excludes the social security contributions which are used for financing the welfare state). It is thus difficult to detect an obvious correlation between a stable tax and a slowed down growth.

In addition, if the link between the tax on labor and employment is direct, that between taxation in general and economic activity is much more diffuse, and is difficult to prove.

Lastly, contrary to what some supply-side economists suggest, public spending is not all destined to be consumed by civil servants. Taxation has, as a counterpart, the provision of public services. Some are very complementary to private production, either by contributing to or supporting them, as may be the case for expenditures related to the judicial system and the police force, and for the infrastructures of transportation and communication, education and health. And even if many of these services could be produced by the private sector, it is abusive to consider that their utility becomes non-existent since they are produced by the State and that under these conditions the tax which is used for financing them is, purely and simply, wasted.

If it is true that taxation lowers the national product below what it could be, on the other hand, the link between taxation and the growth rate is much more complex than the simple version of supply-side economics would suggest. And it could well be insignificant.

The economic theory of taxation is more useful for measuring the specific importance of the distortions that each tax introduces into the economy, and for directing reforms of the tax structure, than as a global explanation of the decline of growth.

From this point of view it is the tax on labor, the financing instrument of the welfare state, which incontestably plays the most harmful part by massively penalizing employment, and consequently the output of companies.

But the thesis of Eurosclerosis, as convincing as it is, is not all that history has shown us. For a firm's level of production is not determined by its costs alone. It also depends on the level of demand. A strong increase in demand makes it possible to increase production and to return a profit even if the cost of labor is increasing.

This aspect is neglected by "traditional" economists and the Eurosclerosis theorists who suppose *a priori* that one cannot act upon demand because they deny the effectiveness of macroeconomic policies. According to them, governments in particular do not have any impact on the demand for goods and services since it is the consumers who direct it in their own fashion, according to their incomes and their preferences.

The macroeconomic analysis resulting from the difficulties of the Great Depression, however, shows quite to the contrary that government financial policies, in terms of currency and budget, significantly affect the overall level of household demand. By supporting the creation of money and spending more than it removes purchasing power from households through taxation, the State can increase overall consumer demand, the global demand directed toward businesses.

Macroeconomic policy thus can be expansive, recessive or neutral. By hitting a dead end on the first two possibilities, the "classical" economists who neglect macroeconomics posit a specific case whose occurrence is not the most probable in real economies. In order to be able to concentrate only on the cost of labor, they would need to prove that the States' macroeconomic management is always perfectly neutral, which it generally is not.

There is an indication of this, when it is observed that the growth rate often changes while at the same time the degree of sclerosis of the labor market remains constant. The macroeconomic policies that affect global demand are likely to vary appreciably from one year to the next. They also follow a different course from one country to another and in one period or another. These different policies differently affect the economies that are subject to identical conditions of international demand and identical production costs. This is why one observes in the same period faster or slower expansion in different countries, in the absence of the modifications of the operating conditions of the welfare State and the labor market.

Thus the monetary and budgetary policies adopted in the United States at the beginning of the Nineties, and in Great Britain, since they returned to a floating exchange rate for the pound sterling, largely diverged from those which were preferred by the continental European governments.

The debate is fundamentally the same today as in the Thirties. The traditional position, that of "the Classics" whom Keynes opposed, denied the responsibility of the monetary and financial policies. The orthodox of those times (and of today), were content to wait until unemployment put enough pressure on wages, leading to reform of the social institutions and regulations, and the conditions of equilibrium would be met again and full employment and growth would return spontaneously. The Keynesians held, on the contrary, that it was especially necessary to change macroeconomic policy and to revitalize activity through budgetary and monetary policies.

This is the controversy that even now pits those economists who criticize restrictive monetary and budgetary policy against those who, close to the central banks, cite the need for structural reform alone, conservative macroeconomic policy being, in their eyes, the only one possible.

To explain the rate of production simply by the excessive level of labor costs, however, constitutes only a partial analysis and one that is, necessarily, likely to fail, except in the very rare circumstances where macroeconomic neutrality is adhered to perfectly. The tradition of blaming the sluggishness of the economy on high wage costs thus draws on an explanation that combines with the fluctuations of demand that affect every business, which the macroeconomists call aggregate demand.

But before turning to the political and macroeconomic dimension of the problem, it is advisable to look at a naive version of the traditional analysis, that which assigns the responsibility for our troubles to the "globalization" of the economy, because of the success that this thesis meets in public opinion, including among the people who run the corporations and the political structure.

"Globalization," A Convenient Scapegoat

The high cost of labor in the European economies would have harmful effects on employment and growth as competition increases from countries with low wages and no social protection systems worthy of the name. Competition from companies with low wage costs would cause the bankruptcy of our companies and the disappearance of the corresponding jobs. Indeed, the price of labor in Europe cannot go down because of the welfare state. But, especially, it could never fall enough to match the level of the developing countries, for European employees quite simply could not live on 5 dollars per day.

Professional economists do not usually share such a pessimistic view. They stress that the wages of the developing countries are not so much lower than ours if one takes into account the respective skill levels. The poor wages of the emerging economies correspond to very poor qualifications, and not all goods and services can be produced with low-skilled labor, which limits the effective competition of the developing countries to low technology products and certain sectors.

In addition, the legal, economic and social environment of these countries is generally rudimentary and not very favorable to firm productivity, which actually limits the relocation possibilities of European plants. A Lyons firm, for these reasons, will go more readily to Ireland or the Czech Republic than to Ghana, India or Malaysia.

Lastly, when development occurs, the local wages increase very quickly to converge toward the corresponding wages of America or Europe, as seen in Japan, Hong Kong, Singapore and today in Korea and China.

Moreover, specialists in international trade long ago established that even if an underdeveloped country had an absolute cost advantage in the production of all the goods and services that a rich country manufactures, it does not follow that it is impossible for the high cost countries to produce anything. Each national economy has an interest in specializing in the production for which its comparative advantage is greatest.

The traditional example of economics textbooks is that of Great Britain and Portugal. The Portuguese are able to produce wine and cloth at a better absolute cost than the British. However, Portugal has an interest to specialize only in the production of wine because that is the sector where its advantage over England is largest. Because of this, the British workers are not deprived of all employment, but the vine growers among them must convert themselves into the production of cloth. However, growth in the textile industry must be fairly strong, or their wage demands rather moderate, for new jobs to be created there. And this returns us to the global conditions of demand and macroeconomic policy mentioned above.

It may be also that the demand for skills in the textile industry is much higher than that in the wine industry. In that case one will observe the opening of the salary range following the re-specialization resulting from international trade.

Thus today's emerging countries tend to specialize in activities which use relatively less skilled labor than the more established industrial countries, because they have an abundance of manual labor with little training while they have few workers with strong qualifications. Conversely, in Europe or the United States, producers using low skilled manual labor hardly have a future. And so it is the least skilled people who encounter the greatest difficulties in the labor market of the rich countries.

The hypothesis is all the more disconcerting since it corresponds indeed to that which one has observed for some twenty years in almost all the industrialized countries, and most markedly in the United States and Great Britain. The income gap between university graduates and the least educated workers has increased greatly.

Under these conditions, by preventing any adjustment, resistance to lowering wages, which especially relates to the most modest wages—those of the least skilled workers—ends up excluding them from employment altogether. The combination of Eurosclerosis and international competition proves as deleterious as it is socially unacceptable.

In the rich countries of continental Europe where the welfare state is omnipresent, the inflexibility of the labor market has limited the rise of inequalities of income but at the same time, for the least qualified, it has increased the difficulty of finding a job. There one finds the conflict between the two growth models of the United States and Europe referred to by Krugman.

Globalization, which is often used as a bogeyman to justify and to defend the welfare state—without which, they tell us, employees would be reduced to misery—thus appears, on the contrary, to be more harmful for the least skilled, the more highly developed the welfare state. It is a paradoxical but fundamental consequence of the traditional diagnosis.

However, if the flexibility of the wage scale is a fact, especially in the countries whose apparatus of income transfer is small, the immense economic literature on this subject hardly shows the proven responsibility of international trade in its development. The majority of economists agree in recognizing that the globalization of the trade is not the factor responsible for the reduction in the lowest wages. It seems, rather, that the phenomenon is due mainly to technical progress, which has increased productivity and the wages of the most qualified to the detriment of the demand for low skilled labor, which is forsaken by employers.

There is thus a real competitive pressure from the poor countries on the wages of the rich countries, but it is limited to a small segment of the working population and to a small number of economic sectors. Its quantitative effects could be limited to approximately a third of the observed drop in the lowest wages, the other two thirds coming from the technical progress that call for stronger qualifications.

For the reduced effect which remains, nevertheless, and for some of the European employees with the least qualifications, this is added to the reduction of employment opportunities resulting from the interference of the welfare state in the labor market, which bring about an increase in the cost of labor.

But these negative effects on growth are probably too minor to be taken into account.

Is the Welfare State the Employees' Sole Defense
Against International Trade?

In counterpoint, a more recent interpretation attempts to justify the development of the welfare state as being made necessary by global-ization. According to Dani Rodrik of Harvard University,[11] the inter-national economists who only emphasize the advantages of the spe-cialization of international trade go too far in ignoring the disadvan-tages which it presents for employees in the rich countries.

First of all, the relocation of activities which it entails increases job insecurity, diminishes workers' nonpecuniary advantages, and weak-ens the trade unions which defend their interests. In the second place, it destroys the social standards of labor which guaranteed certain rights to the workers. None of that is taken into account in statistics on the national product. Finally, it makes it increasingly difficult for govern-ments to finance the social guarantees which contribute to protecting employees against the major- risks.

These disadvantages would explain the development of the welfare state parallel to the opening up of the economy, by the need to com-pensate the most underprivileged for the disadvantages. It is known that States' share, in the broadest sense, including the programs of in-come transfers, went from 20% of the GNP, on average, before the last World War to 47% today in the wealthy countries. Which, ac-cording to Rodrik, corresponds to protection against the risks related to international trade.

But when the factors of production become more mobile as is the case today, and precisely because of the international openness, it is more difficult for the governments to raise taxes. Then it is not possi-ble to go further in developing the compensatory actions of the State because of the tax crisis, which has been intensifying for the last two decades. It follows that the continuation of globalization now presents employees with increased risks, without anything in return. And these increased risks are even combined, for the least qualified, with lower pay.

One can, however, question the reality of the relationship postulated between the opening up of the economy and the size of the welfare state. The majority of the expenses of this last relates to payment for pensions and health care coverage for employees, services which have nothing to do with international trade. These risks are not related to globalization.

One can also show that the rise of the welfare state has nothing to do with opening up the economies. In America as in Europe, it is a social invention that was developed in response to the difficulties generated by the Depression of the Thirties, which occurred precisely during a period of increased protectionism. In the same way, a healthy portion of the expenses of the welfare state goes to retirees who benefit from the low prices of imports but do not fear for their employment.

One can thus recognize that globalization exerts negative effects on the well-being of employed workers, and that, combined with the inflexibility of wages, it makes the employment of some of the least qualified a little more difficult, although this last effect is more probably due to technical progress. On the other hand it unquestionably accentuates the difficulties of financing the welfare state, but since it leads from this fact to reducing the tax on labor (which, together with the economic situation, is a factor that aggravates unemployment), it is rather likely to affect employment positively.

It should not be forgotten either that international openness plays a very positive role. It contributes incontestably to increasing the average standard of living, as the classical theory of international specialization would have it and as contemporary studies on the factors of growth show it to be.[12]

We will come back to the problems of the welfare state. But it should be emphasized here again how little use the traditional diagnosis can be that stresses the permanent overly high cost of labor, even if it is perfectly relevant to explaining structural unemployment, in explaining the short term fluctuations of employment and unemployment. It constitutes, at best, only a partial diagnosis. Indeed, it neglects a more natural explanation that holds with the analysis of governmental financial, monetary and tax policies, which it supposes are always given and fixed, and perfectly neutral, to assign all the responsibility for slow growth and unemployment only to the inflexibility of the labor market.

It thus consolidates the position of those who want to maintain the course of strict and unchanged monetary and financial policies and who are devoted to reducing taxes and national expenditure, with growth then having to return on its own—as soon as the real wages have dropped.

Macroeconomic Responsibility

For the end of growth and the advent of permanent unemployment in Europe are, in fact, explained by this disinflationary policy implemented at the beginning of the Eighties and then reactivated, after a brief interlude of recovery at the end of the decade, by the Bundesbank's restrictive policy.

Conservative monetary policies have a secondary effect of driving up the currency exchange rate and penalizing exporters as well as domestic producers, who are then faced with increased competition from imports whose prices have gone down. That generates fear, an unfounded fear of "globalization." Actually, competition from the poor countries is irresistible not because of their low wages. More to the point is that our products are too expensive, and our wages also, insofar as their domestic price does not change, or in any case not instantaneously, with the increase in the exchange rate. It is our currencies' rates of exchange that penalize export, bolster imports particularly from emerging countries, and make our wages prohibitive compared to those of foreign countries.

Real wage rigidity thus only aggravates the situation by making the economy particularly sensitive and allergic to any episode of disinflation, which then results automatically in a strong increase in unemployment. Whereas in the Thirties it was an erroneous monetary policy of the United States, and the Gold Standard in Europe, that transformed the stock exchange crash into an international economic debacle,[13] in the Eighties, the desire to fight double-digit inflation, initially, following the two oil crises of 1974 and 1979, and in the Nineties the Deutsche mark standard, took the responsibility for the slowdown.

The Treaty of Maastricht which instituted this new system of fixed exchange rates in Europe will appear in the textbooks of history as the error or, worse still, the fault of 1991, in the same way as there were the deflationary policies of the Thirties, and in particular in those countries of the gold standard. As in the Thirties, the tensions would quickly appear insupportable to several countries. Spain, Great Britain and Italy gave up the Deutsche mark standard and led to the exchange rate crisis at the end of 1992, only one year after the signing of the Treaty, as others had quickly left the gold standard.

And as in the Thirties, these days, the countries that gave up the Deutsche mark standard came out ahead of those who stubbornly clung to it, including France. Those who clung to the mark standard or the gold standard had to take the full brunt of declining growth and the rise of unemployment while the "devaluationists" saw their growth restored and unemployment fall, without any notable inflationary consequence nor continuous or catastrophic depreciation of their currency.

Complementary Analyses and the Sequence of Reforms

On the whole, the three explanations of the weak European performance in the early Eighties and the beginning of the Nineties are not mutually contradictory but are complementary.

The hypothesis of economic maturity explains the greater difficulty nowadays of finding high growth rates. These imply heavier capital expenditures and more resolute and more profound restructuring of firms, which only serves to underscore the need for good macroeconomic policies. Such policies would enable us to go on with the expansion, a condition for resuming investment, for the alleviation of unemployment due to the economic circumstances and for initiating the essential reform of the welfare state.

This latter effect, in its turn, by giving flexibility back to the labor market and reducing the rigidity of wages, as well as by reducing the tax cost of labor, makes it possible to accelerate the restructuring of firms, and supports growth. But it can be conceived only during a time of expansion, the reforming surgery being acceptable by the public only in a context of increased pay and proliferation of employment opportunities.

Thus, it is not a question of choosing one policy to the exclusion of another, but of putting them into action simultaneously because they are mutually reinforcing. Changes to the macroeconomic policy and structural reform go hand in hand.[14]

The countries that succeeded to re-establish the equilibrium of their public finances in a lasting way are those that went ahead with spending cuts, in particular in the systems of redistribution, rather than with increasing the tax burden, and that did so during a time of economic expansion rather than during a phase of contraction or recession.

So it is necessary to reorient the macro-economic policy and at the same time to relieve the economy of its structural rigidities. The two policies are complementary.

However, making these moves simultaneously is politically too difficult. It is more realistic to determine a prioritized sequence of changes. Still, structural reform by itself cannot cause a renewal of growth in an economy where the global demand is suppressed. There is no example of such a success, and in addition it proves much more difficult to carry out major structural reforms in an economy in contraction or slow growth than in an economy undergoing strong expansion.

There are certainly counterexamples, such as the cases of the formerly communist countries and New Zealand, which carried out major, even revolutionary structural reforms, while adopting macroeconomic policies of austerity, thus combining reform and recession. But those were examples of the type of economy that had already broken down because of the tax crisis and the dissolution of the previous economic system (the USSR and Eastern Europe), that is to say, of a country whose essential resources came from goods and services which were threatened by the development of international competition, and whose economy was indeed on the brink of collapse.

Against a chronic background of crisis lasting nearly twenty years, it is neither possible nor particularly desirable to wait until the Euro-conservative economies break down to undertake to reform them. It is necessary to revitalize growth first, which is only possible through a suitable macroeconomic policy, in order to put oneself in a position then to approach the difficult task of reforming the State structures under politically acceptable conditions.

The analysis of good monetary and budgetary policies is thus at the heart of the debate, the more so as the doctrine currently most widely disseminated, "Euro-monetarism," sends the continental economies off in a dramatically wrong direction compared to the present needs.

Unfortunately, "politically correct thinking," i.e. the insufficiency of preliminary reflection, the absence of open democratic debate and the exclusive appeal made to government experts, hence the mass of official propaganda, have locked the national leadership into an economic dead end which has translated into and will continue to result in repeated electoral failures.

DOCTRINAL ROADBLOCKS

Doctrinal roadblocks are a French weakness that constitutes an old and constant tradition of the Ministry of Finance. That was Valéry Giscard d'Estaing's attitude in the Sixties, for whom "there was no other policy," only that of the government to which he belonged. He was not alone in this, the practice was intensified still more by Bercy, in spite of the about-face and the vicissitudes of the socialist presidencies. It is tending today to become European, the Euro-monetarist policy usually being presented as the only solution that can be applied to the continent's economic problems.

Is it conceivable to change the monetary and budgetary policy? Is this possible? Is this even desirable? Aren't we following the only reasonable policy? And besides, isn't it dictated to us by the tyranny of the international financial markets? Here is the litany of "the economically correct" thinkers of the Nineties.

In a variation on the theory of globalization, our experts and central bankers assure us that indeed the international opening of the financial markets henceforth imposes a completely conservative monetary and financial policy on the national governments.

Insofar as the latter constantly need to borrow for themselves and to support the upsurge of capital from the whole world to finance the companies, they compete with one another to get their hands on the savings of the Japanese, the Americans, of the Gulf countries and South America. Countries with low inflation and a stable rate of exchange inspire confidence and thus profit from a competitive advantage as borrowers, since they guarantee to international lenders an unchanged value of their investment at the time of settlement.

There is thus no margin of error for the national economic policy makers because any inflation or any variation of the parity of exchange rate would be refused by the lenders and would immediately cause an international capital flight, an increased depreciation of the exchange rate leading to more inflation and an additional depreciation of the currency, in an endless spiral. Hyperinflation and economic collapse would be at the end of the road.

Even if we suppose that one could stop before this fatal crash, stronger inflation or an unstable exchange rate would be enough to make some of the capital flee and would require that the rate of remuneration to lenders be raised by a premium to account for the risk factor, to persuade them to keep their capital in the country. And in the end, that would certainly penalize the government and the companies of the inflationary economy.

This apocalyptic vision is however doubly, and incredibly, false. First of all because the risk premium does not necessarily increase the real cost of capital, or not to a significant degree. It compensates only for the risks of depreciation, if the financial markets are efficient, which specialized economists and the better-informed experts usually tend to recognize as a proven fact.

Second, because there is a whole gamut of more or less expansionist macroeconomic policies and not all of them necessarily lead to either inflation nor to continued depreciation of the exchange rate. It is a gross caricature—which it is scandalous to hear from the lips of well-informed political leaders—to deny the existence of *various* noninflationary policies, as if there were on one side a multiplicity of inflationary policies and, on the other, only one policy that would be noninflationary.

A government can actually practice a wide variety of more or less inflationary policies, as the diversity of the rates of inflation proves, even among just the OECD countries. And a bit of inflation does not inevitably go hand in hand with lower growth, as various recent examples show, particularly in Great Britain, the United States and in Italy before the recent return to a forced convergence toward the Deutsche mark. On the contrary, there can be excessively disinflationary policies that end up one day falling into deflation.

Consequently the "tyranny of the markets" does not definitively dictate the behavior of the monetary policy of governments. The latter can fix their nominal short term interest rates, move toward such and such inflation rate, let the exchange rate appreciate or be depreciated according to their financial and tax choices, as they like. The market makers are satisfied to set corresponding risk premiums on the loans.

It is only when one government decides to fix the parity of its currency that it submits itself to "the tyranny" of the markets. Indeed, the tendency of the exchange rates, like that of all other prices, is to fluctuate according to the economic conditions that vary from one day to another, month by month. To fix a price unilaterally, and necessarily arbitrarily, means giving lenders and borrowers an opportunity to speculate because they know by experience that the economic conditions will change and that consequently, one day or another, the price will have to do the same.

Stasis does not exist in economics or in finance, any more than in the world of living in general. To fix a price, the external price of a currency in this case, is an open invitation to speculation that makes it possible to make huge profits if one can correctly forecast the differential between the currency's future equilibrium point and its current managed price.

As the rate of exchange between two currencies depends chiefly on the difference of the inflation rates of the two countries concerned, administratively setting the exchange rate immediately obliges the government that decides it to maintain an inflation rate similar to that of the partner country. Otherwise, speculation breaks out in anticipation of a future and inevitable adjustment of the exchange rate that will reflect the differences in inflation.

When this happens, the government that no longer is successful in controlling the exchange rate denounces an "attack" by speculators, or the "unbearable pressure" of the markets. It is a "tyranny" exerted against its will which is, of course, looking to the higher interests of the country. That is exactly how it was in the era, fortunately bygone, of administrative control of all the prices, which claimed to be fighting against inflation by controlling businesses and trade allegedly in defense of the consumer. One day the administrative price-fixing was abolished, and nothing happened in terms of inflation. We later learned that, in fact, inflation depended on the government's monetary and budgetary policy and not on those plotting speculators, grocers and service providers that all the political leaders and the financial civil servants had been castigating for years.

This is the same scenario that is starting up again with the international price of currency, which plays an essential role in an economy open to the outside, whereas in the Fifties and Sixties, in a more closed economy, it was the internal price of money (the general level of prices, i.e. the price of all the goods and services) which was the primary focus of our governments.

The "tyranny" that the markets exert on the monetary and budgetary policy thus exists only insofar as the government intends to maintain a fixed exchange rate compared to a foreign currency, or any other arbitrary criterion such as, for example, the price of an ounce of gold.

It is in this only sense that the market exerts its monitoring: it watches over a precise relationship that the national governments are perfectly free to take on or not to take on. If the monetary authorities allowed the currency purely and simply to float, the "dictatorship" of the international financial markets would disappear overnight.

So it is the choice of a specific monetary policy that causes the tyranny of the markets. As it happens, it is a question of a policy of "definitively" fixing the exchange rate with a neighboring currency, together with an objective of zero inflation. This policy is extreme, given the very vast range of policies that could be selected. Presented without valid rationale as the only possible choice, it corresponds to the rigid choice of monetary "fundamentalism," an excessive version and illegitimate offshoot of the monetarist theory.

Economic difficulties usually give rise, after a slight delay, to theories intended to guide governments in a complex environment. But these guides for action in a specific context prove generally circumstantial while they naturally tend to be transformed into doctrines pretending to timeless applicability, which adapt only slowly to the new conditions and the problems that they cause.

The Great Depression had led theorists and governments to design and institute monetary and budgetary policies to stimulate global demand. These were changed, after the war, into macroeconomic policies that claimed to be able to succeed in permanently managing a "fine tuning" of growth, without inflation or unemployment. The vanity of the attempt was made clear at the time of the great inflation that began to take off in the middle the Sixties and exploded in the Seventies. The new context caused the popular success of monetarist analyses that stressed the responsibility of monetary policies in the growth of inflation. This theory, convincingly confirmed by abundant studies and accepted today by all economists, generated in its turn a great mistrust with regard to any expansionist monetary policy.

But, as so often happens, they went too far in adjusting the balance. The experiment with too-relaxed monetary policies in the Sixties led, in reaction, to a criticism of any soft money policy. The fight against inflation had become the absolute priority, and often the single objective of macroeconomic policy.

Unfortunately the financial conservatism which was followed and was adopted wholesale in the closed world of government functionaries and central bank management outlived the end of inflation that came in the second half of the Eighties. Thus we have prolonged the use of anti-inflation measures in economies where inflation has practically disappeared and where it is deflation that is the real threat.

Worse yet, combined with the doctrines of fixed exchange rates and the intention to rebuild in Europe a Bretton Woods-type system (given up by the United States and other major countries in 1971), and then a single currency, this anti-inflationary eagerness led to the implementation of Germany's monetary ultra-conservatism in every country, reinforced beyond the Rhine by the need to fight the inflationary consequences of the German reunification of 1989. The Euro plan that was launched in this context thus came at the worst moment.

But the new monetarism, which is based on rigorous observation of the link between expansionist policies and inflation, and which actually does not tell us much about what should be the preferred level of inflation, was transformed imperceptibly into a doctrine of fighting against any inflation, whatever the level. And now the objective of these new macroeconomic doctrines is zero inflation, the theoretical justification of which rests on very fragile premises. We have thus gone from the scientific observation of the monetary causes of inflation to the dogma of monetary conservatism, which has more followers in Europe than in the United States.

The Attack against Expansionist Policies

Monetarism is a scientific analysis that assigns immediate responsibility for inflation to the creation of money. According to monetarists, there is no significant period of inflation that is not accompanied by a strong money creation. This assertion can be regarded today as largely proven.

The monetarists also add that governments are responsible for monetary creation through the interest rates policies, which is also little disputed. And they conclude by emphasizing that one cannot trust political leaders to guarantee price stability, for there is always strong temptation to distribute money to build temporary purchasing power, for the benefit of those electoral customers who profit from the public transfers; at least as long as price increases resulting from the increased money supply has not taken away from consumers the additional purchasing power thus created.

In the long term, monetarists say, this creation of currency serves no purpose. It does not create additional wealth but only fuels price increases across the board. It cannot accelerate the rate of economic growth, except in a transitory way. It does not have a lasting effect on the real economic activity.

This last assertion is much disputed. However, certain monetarist authors go even further and affirm that in the long term inflation is not only ineffective or "neutral," it may be harmful in that it would contribute to reducing real growth[15].

In the current state of the debate this assertion is not proven. In the long term, inflation's effect on growth is not clear and, in fact, it often proves positive. However, over shorter periods and in the event of recession or of slowdowns, it is scarcely debatable that monetary stimulation plays a positive role. And the defenders of expansionist macroeconomic policies never had the long term in mind: their concern is to bring the economy out of temporary recessions as quickly as possible. Their perspective is short term. And it may be appropriate to act to improve the economy's short-term prospects if that does not entail a long-term cost that is greater than the immediate benefit.

It should not be forgotten, either, that governments can be mistaken in practicing excessive monetary restriction. That is Milton Friedman's analysis of the reasons behind the severity of the Great Depression of the Thirties. He shows that on this occasion a too-restrictive monetary policy can stop real growth and cause considerable damage. And all the recent works on the question confirm the decisive and negative role of restrictive monetary policies in the drop that the industrial economies experienced during the Thirties.

Many authors have shown in recent years that anti-inflation policies reduce the growth of the real economy at the same time. There is hardly ever any disinflation without deceleration of activity, and thus without increased unemployment due to the economic situation. Disinflation is always costly.

However, those who hold to the new financial conservatism, undoubtedly in keeping with the spirit of the circumstances of the high priority fight against the inflation in the Seventies, take account of only one aspect of the analysis of monetary policies, the negative side. They want to eradicate inflation, purely and simply, without thinking the least bit about the danger of excessive monetary restriction. This asymmetrical vision of reality was all the more devastating to the European economies because it combined two unfounded beliefs: the superiority of zero inflation and that of fixed systems of exchange.

Two Unfounded Beliefs

Indeed, to the proof of governmental responsibility regarding money supply and inflation, the monetary fundamentalists have added these two beliefs which have no scientific basis.

According to them, the best inflation now is zero inflation. And they like this doctrine all the more, since it constitutes a convenient objective criterion of good monetary management. In their eyes, it is better to have automatic management of the monetary policy, which can then be entrusted to independent technicians, rather than to leave governments to govern liquidity according to the circumstances, for one cannot trust them to limit themselves to non-inflationary money creation.

However, the desirability of zero inflation is not a recognized scientific assertion but an assumption or a belief, just like the assertion that inflation may at best have no effect on growth, and more probably a negative effect.

These postulates are reinforced by the analyses of the extreme monetarists of the school known as "rational anticipation," which suppose that managing inflation has no a real effect on economic activity in the short term, either. That means two things, important but false: first of all that increasing the money supply cannot stimulate expansion, even temporarily. And at the same time, symmetrically, a disinflationary policy will have no costs in terms of slowing down activity. Consequently, since manipulating the inflation level has no economic cost, the inflation rate can be selected arbitrarily by the government. And as its long term effects on the growth are, they say, negative, then why not choose a level of zero price increases since that does not harm prosperity, quite to the contrary.

Since the only enemy would be inflation, the permanent, even sole, objective of macroeconomic policy must be to reduce it. That is what virtue consists of. Growth will come as a bonus. And if the economy suffers, that would be due to its not being "flexible" enough and to undue resistance from employees. It is necessary to re-educate them in the morals of effort and hard work: "No pain, no gain."

The extreme monetarist doctrines, or "monetary fundamentalism," to use Edward Luttwak's term,[16] thus go beyond that which the scientific argumentation of Friedmanesque monetarism shows. It posit zero inflation as an objective with the misunderstanding of the negative short term consequences on expansion considered nonexistent, and recommends entrusting monetary management to a technical power independent of the elected governments, a central bank for example, without worrying any further about the very real effects of monetary management.

The Keynesians, on the other hand, always maintained that monetary creation, even when accompanied by a certain rise of prices, had positive effects on growth, at least when the economy does not fully use its production potential and when the prices are "rigid," that is, are not adjusted instantaneously when the rate of currency creation increases. And they agree in fact with Milton Friedman in recognizing that restrictive monetary policy can create recession, and thus *a fortiori* a simple slowdown of economic growth.

The Obsession with Fixed Exchange Rates

In Europe, and especially in France, the new fundamentalism of zero inflation meets up with another monetary obsession, the belief in the absolute superiority, under all circumstances, of the system of fixed exchange rates. There is an astonishing constancy of attitude on this matter among our financial elites.[17] Already in 1933, at the international economic conference of London, the delegates of the gold standard bloc, led by France, attributed all the evils of the time to the absence of a healthy currency whereas those from the other countries stressed, rightly, the need for a policy of monetary reflation and economic expansion.

This was a constant theme too, for more than half a century, from Jacques Rueff, a high-ranking civil servant very representative of the milieu close to the French Ministry of Finance–that a hard currency plays an essential role in guaranteeing the stability of society. Thus the French leadership passed from the ideology of the gold franc to that of the strong franc, and from the gold standard to the Deutsche mark-standard. Conversely Great Britain, which had chosen with pragmatism and wisdom to abandon the fixed exchanges and the gold standard in 1931, opportunely did so again in 1992 by quickly renouncing fixed parity with the Deutsche mark.

In the Europe of the Eighties, monetary conservatism thus took on a specific tonality, based on alignment with the Deutsche mark. Indeed, because of its past, disastrous, experiences of inflation, and the experience of independence from the Bundesbank together with an unwavering pursuit of price stability, Germany appears to be an example of excellence in monetary conservatism.

Seeking fixed exchange rates vis-a-vis the Deutsche mark, then the plan to create a single currency by merging the national currencies with it, together with a more or less explicit agreement on joint "German style" monetary management, in fact means disseminating the model of monetary fundamentalism to all the European countries.

This is "Euro-monetarism," a doctrine that consists in setting up a system of exchange rates that returns Europe to a Deutsche mark standard, as there was formerly a gold standard. It defines a new "monetary constitution" for the continent that gets around the current operation of democratic policy.

The Germans attach to the mark the essence of their national pride, which could not be expressed on the political level since the last war. And as they fear the warm water of moderated inflation (having been scalded on several occasions by hyperinflation), they accept the union only on their own economic and monetary conditions. Thus they require their partners in the management of the future single currency to prove the seriousness of their commitment by adhering always to the conservative criteria of the Bundesbank. For that, before unification, the Euro candidate countries' currencies had to become as strong as the Deutsche mark, for central bankers and the public opinion of Germany cannot give up the mark for a less secure currency.

Based on this fact, Germany is exporting its own view of monetary policy to all its partners in the European system of fixed exchange rates that takes the place, on our continent, of the world system of Bretton Woods. The Euro-monetarist policy that results from adopting the Deutsche mark standard determines an inflation approaching zero, which is not suited to the real needs of contemporary economies in which the risk is not too much, but too little, inflation.

CONCLUSION

The responsibilities for the sluggishness of the economies of continental Europe are known. They find their principal source in the attempt to construct the Euro and in the monetary and financial conservatism that accompanies it and justifies it. One even begins to say it
openly, on the right as on the left, and among even the most savage
Euro-partisans, in spite of the official taboo on debate.

The governments engaged in this enterprise and the fundamentalist
governors of the central banks have until now eluded criticism by lay-
ing the blame on the welfare state system of redistribution and the lack
of flexibility in the labor markets. The diagnosis is not inaccurate but
it is incomplete, as is testified by the fact that the welfare state and
wage rigidities did not prevent the resumption of growth in France at
the end of the Eighties and again in 1993-1994, when the government,
for electoral reasons, gave up the budgetary policy of deflation.

If we set aside the whimsical scapegoats like globalization of the
economy or the "tyranny of the financial markets" and the excessive
emphasis on the impotence of monetary policy, there remains as an
explanation of European under-performance only the blind accession
to an extreme Euro-monetarist policy, or of monetary fundamentalism.

This policy that preaches zero inflation and fixed exchanges imposes upon us, by means of the Deutsche mark standard, the adoption
of the German economic policy. That results in pointless and debili-
tating disinflation and budgetary austerity that can be only self-
destructive in a period of economic deceleration.

In this sense Maastricht is responsible for our woes because the
Treaty reflected the German requirements of financial conservatism in
exchange for abandoning the mark in favor of the euro. One could
economically, but certainly not politically, conceive a different monetary union leading to a weak euro, or at least somewhere between the

lira and the mark. Such a euro would have resembled the French franc, it would be hard to tell the difference, and such is, indeed, the secret dream which our representatives cherish.

However, we had to yield to the demands of the Germans. So just like the gold standard in the Thirties, the Deutsche mark standard of today causes economic devastation on the continent. And that unfortunately will not be limited to the duration of the German rebuilding of the Länder of the East.

Indeed, the single currency is and will remain a harmful enterprise for the European economies. For this reason it cannot be launched, or it will explode sooner or later—as we will see in the following chapter.

Contrary to what the fundamentalists would like us to believe, establishing the single currency will not put an end to stagnation because its management will continue to rest on the same concepts. So we have the prospect of an enduring mediocrity of economic growth awaiting Europe in the next years. Decline appears inescapable. One need look no further for the causes of the distress so perceptible on the continent, whereas optimism reigns in the economies that have resumed growth, on the other side of the Atlantic and, closer to us, on other side of the English Channel.

Most serious is that this bleeding serves no purpose. It is based on an economic error and *a priori* policies, just like the deflation of the Thirties. Badly conceived plans, shortsighted policies in spite of the grandiose claim of constructing a new currency and a continental State, the refusal to recognize the basic economic mechanisms and the mistakes of economic policy, accompanied by intimidation of public opinion. The European mistake of the Nineties is this century's most serious error of economic policy after that of the Thirties. The liabilities of the governments are particularly heavy, their behavior inept and their responsibility immense.

Chapter II

THE SINGLE CURRENCY
VERSUS
THE ECONOMY

The monetary policy in Europe is dictated today by the exchange rate target that the Deutsche mark standard represents. It imposes disinflation on economies which, unlike Germany, are not experiencing inflationary tensions. The effects on real activity, production and unemployment, are serious. This chapter explains the single currency's harmful effects on the economy and shows how it is opposed, over the long haul, to the pursuit of prosperity.

In the present circumstances, managing the French franc the way the mark is managed involves (as a consequence of the permanent disinflation that it induces), a prohibitive cost for the French economy. Which is also happening, for the same reasons, in other European countries, Italy for example.

But this penalizing policy will not come to an end with the establishment of the single currency, if it is carried out. Indeed, even in principle, the euro constitutes an economic error. Europe is not an "optimal monetary zone," i.e. a geographical zone in which it is advantageous for the national economies to fix their exchange rates or, to take the concept of fixed exchange rates to its logical conclusion, to replace several national currencies with a single currency.

A single currency is not necessarily nor equally appropriate to several national economies, in particular because the inflation rate for full employment may be different in each of the concerned countries, but also because of the structural differences which separate the national economies in significant ways. The mobility of labor, the concentration of the external trade and the sectoral distribution of business activity remain indeed dissimilar from one economy to another, and the intensification of the exchanges results in amplifying these differences rather than reducing them.

That being said, a single monetary policy, and which furthermore is absurdly encumbered with arbitrary and uniform constraints on budgetary matters—those of the so-called "stability pact" imposed by Germany—will continue to inflict significant and completely pointless costs on the nations embarking on this adventure.

Moreover, the leaders of the countries concerned, that is first and foremost those of France and Germany, understand these difficulties very well and try to cut corners with their partners' requirements. Each one attempts to impose its own conception of the monetary policy. The natural divergence of the national monetary policies consequently introduces an element of permanent political conflict between partner States within a monetary zone that is inherently less than optimal.

Then it is crucial to know which member State will see its monetary views prevail. This controversy over what should be the management of the European Central Bank first surfaced at the time of the Summit of Dublin. France revealed its real preferences by requiring that, besides fighting against a now non-existent inflation, the future single monetary policy concern itself with growth and employment, by putting the directors of the future European Central Bank under the effective control of the national governments. Which amounts to tempering the exclusively anti-inflationary objective defined in Maastricht that authorized a technocratic monetary management, independent of politics.

Any requirement other than monetary stability, however, seemed to be unacceptable to German public opinion and to the management of the Bundesbank. Thus the creation of a single currency raises several contradictory questions which inevitably come to the fore as the due date approaches. Which monetary policy will win out? How will the losers be compensated? And for the sake of which purported mutual advantages? It is a shame, at the very least, that this essential debate comes up so tardily, when it should have been started well before the process was begun.

What will be the outcome of this political war for monetary power, whose costs the citizens of the member States are paying today? The language of the governments is that of resolution and irreversibility. But it causes a sinking feeling and a growing skepticism in public opinion and among businesses.

Can we still escape the euro trap? Beyond official speeches, it is necessary to trust in the economic realities. When a policy is unnecessarily expensive and when the cost to the community keeps growing, it ends up being abandoned. The euro, not being viable, will not be created, or if it is it will not last.

But in politics, as in economics, the principle of uncertainty reigns. Nobody can predict the date when an event will take place, even if its occurrence is beyond doubt. This is why it is impossible to say whether the euro plan will be abandoned even before the date planned for its creation, or some time afterwards. What is certain is that the sooner this happens, the better.

THE COST OF THE DEUTSCHE MARK STANDARD

Monetary fundamentalism ascribes all the evils from which our economies suffer to the absence of a "healthy" currency, that is, of a hard currency, which has the tendency to be revalued. From this point of view, pegging the value of the franc on that of the mark should lead the French economy to prosperity since the mark's exchange rate tends to appreciate relative to that of all the other currencies. Unfortunately, nothing like that has been observed. Quite to the contrary: since the agreement of Maastricht which provides for the final setting of the franc-mark parity, a prelude to the merger into a new currency, one observes a sluggishness of activity and a seemingly irresistible increase in unemployment. The Deutsche mark standard is costing France and some others deeply.

Instead of reinvigorating these economies, as the fundamentalist doctrine would have it, the hard currency is choking them. Actually, contrary to what the euro-monetarists maintain, the evidence shows that monetary management affects the real economy. Money supply can stimulate business activity when it is made more abundant, but it slows down growth when it is diminished. A too restrictive monetary policy will play against the economy.

However, in an open economy, fixing the rate of exchange determines the monetary policy.

A strong exchange rate, that is, a policy of overvaluation or revaluation of the currency, is called a restrictive, disinflationist or deflationary monetary policy, depending on its intensity. By choosing the Deutsche mark standard one necessarily brings along the German monetary policy which has as its object to fight the inflationary tensions beyond the Rhine. Growth in France is strangled together with that in the other countries of the mark zone.

The debates on monetary theory of recent years lead to a conclusion that is, to tell the truth, rather simple. If one judges by observing the real economies, traditional monetarism has it right: currency acts on prices. It is the rate of monetary growth that determines inflation or disinflation. But on the other hand, extreme monetarism is errone-ous: currency is not neutral with respect to production and employ-ment. By its influence on price levels and inflation, it also affects real activity. It stimulates or slows down growth, increasing or reducing unemployment at the same time.

Disinflation is thus necessarily accompanied by a deceleration of growth, while deflation is likely to drive the economy into a depres-sion of major proportions.

If the monetary policy in a closed economy is defined almost ex-clusively by the choice of interest rates which the central bank applies at its discretion to the short term financing market, in an open econ-omy it derives at the same time from the exchange rate that is directly dependent on the level of the interest rates of intervention.

Instead of being the sign of modern liberalism, defending a fixed franc-to-mark parity, i.e. having the monetary authorities set the exter-nal price of the currency, the exchange rate, falls under the planned economy tradition of price control policies.

This means continuing, in an open economy, to control the domes-tic price of money, i.e. the prices of all the goods and services, which has long constituted the ultimate bastion of state intervention in a closed economy. But as this external intervention simultaneously de-termines the monetary policy within a country, it entails far more frightening consequences for the economy than would the direct ad-ministrative control of individual prices.

The thing is that the quantity of currency in circulation decisively affects production and employment, a proposition that is at the center of the controversies surrounding the euro and the monetary unification of Europe. In the final analysis, the success or failure of the single currency depends on the influence that it is able to exert on production and employment.

Does Money Matter?

Many contemporary monetarists have tried to show that money does not affect production or employment. They assert that it would affect only prices and inflation. This extreme hypothesis, known as the neutrality of money, supposes in fact that all prices are perfectly flexible and instantaneously adapt to any adjustment in the quantity of currency in circulation. In reality, things do not happen that way. Prices and wages, i.e. the price of labor, are not perfectly flexible and consequently money is not neutral. This is why monetary policy matters.

The years of high inflation contributed to casting doubt on the utility and on the wisdom of governmental policies. Following Milton Friedman, the "classical" monetarists established that the growth of the money supply in circulation was the direct source of inflation. And as double-digit inflation seemed eminently harmful to the correct operation of the economy, and as it is very costly to eliminate once it settles in, it was concluded that it would be better to practice, permanently, a restrictive monetary policy in order to prevent the return of such inflation. Monetary and financial conservatism became the criterion of good management by governments and by the governors of central banks.

This new doctrine of financial conservatism found its first bases in the theory of the "natural" (or structural") rate of unemployment[1]. According to this analysis, the amount of currency circulating in an economy influences the level of production and consumption only in the short term. In the medium- and long-term, money's real effect becomes less clear. Money does act on the prices but remains basically neutral with respect to business activity. This would mean that on a practical level the government can choose any monetary policy, and consequently any rate of inflation, without disadvantage for the economy since growth and employment do not depend on it.

This analysis contradicts the former report that showed, in the Sixties, an inverse relation between inflation and unemployment. A little more inflation made it possible to reduce unemployment by accelerating the growth of production and thus of the employment offered by companies. Conversely, reducing inflation slowed down growth and increased unemployment.

The governments at that time had a whole range of macroeconomic policies. They could reduce unemployment by stimulating the inflation that stronger growth engendered, or conversely they could seek disinflation that reduced activity while increasing unemployment. This familiar observation was baptized "the Phillips Curve," named for the New Zealand economist who first studied it systematically[2].

The monetarists, however, refined the analysis. They show that the additional creation of money translates into an increase in households' purchasing power only if the prices do not increase by the same proportion. In the same way, companies are encouraged to increase their production of wealth only as long as wages do not increase as quickly as the market demand for their products. This means that monetary growth will have real effects on production and employment only if the prices and the wages are sufficiently rigid, stable, vis-à-vis the growth of the circulation of currency.

In the contrary case, if prices and wages follow the growth of the money supply instantaneously, increasing prices at the same time as incomes, consumer purchasing power remains constant. They do not buy more. For companies, the selling prices will have increased but so will have wage costs. There is thus no reason to produce more. Production does not change. Employment does not change either, and unemployment does not vary. The policy of monetary expansion does not exert an effect on the real economy.

However, the monetarists tell us, consumers and companies learn quickly and consequently they react to government monetarist policies. When they understand the mechanism of inflation they will defend themselves by adjusting prices and wages upwards. Which cancels out the stimulative effects of the initial price increase. Production will return to its former level and unemployment too.

After the momentary surprise, monetary creation will not exert any effect on real equilibriums. Therefore, after a fairly short time, generally speaking, money has no influence on growth and unemployment. In that case the level of unemployment observed, tied to the growth of production, must in the long run be independent of the fluctuations of inflation. And it is observed that over intervals of several years there is practically no link between the rates of inflation and the average growth rates.

Greater monetary creation leads to more inflation but does not have a lasting effect on unemployment. That remains at its "structural" or "natural" level, which depends on labor market regulations and the generosity of the compensation systems but not on the macroeconomic policy. This rate evolves over the course of time rather slowly under the influence of demography, the creation and disappearance of companies, and the microeconomic policies and transfers which affect labor supply and demand.

Under these conditions, governments can do as they like, arbitrarily, as regards monetary policy and rate of inflation. The latter must be judged only on its intrinsic virtues or its disadvantages, since it affects neither production nor growth.

It would appear, then, that in itself inflation offers no advantage but only disadvantages. Each one who anticipates inflation tries to minimize his cash holdings to avoid the depreciation of his liquid assets. And that involves a real cost—a loss of wealth. Cash is useful. Everyone has an interest in maintaining some liquidity. Reducing one's holding to the bare minimum complicates daily life, constantly obliges one to make treasury calculations, to devote time to cash management, time which is taken away from more productive or more pleasant activities. Inflation thus causes a loss of well-being compared to what would be possible to obtain in its absence. It also has as a possible, and undesirable real effect, causing a redistribution of incomes to the detriment of the least skillful: those who do not make these calculations rather quickly become victims of the tax of inflation, to the profit of those who are more skillful in anticipating price increases.

Actually, however, when the economists try to quantify these disadvantages they arrive at extremely low sums, on the order of less than a tenth of a percent of the national product. It could thus seem quite excessive to spell out a country's entire monetary policy to avoid disadvantages that one has hardly managed to identify. But for those who believe in monetary conservatism, it does not matter whether these disadvantages are serious or negligible for, inflation having no real advantage, even its tiny cost constitutes a dead loss. It thus becomes rational to fight any inflation under any circumstances.

In this case zero inflation should be the best. For some, even, it would be advisable to seek negative inflation, as Milton Friedman in his theory on the optimal money supply suggests. For negative inflation constitutes the only practical means to remunerate the holders of cash, which has an economic utility and must be encouraged by payment of positive interest (income). However, it is impossible to pay interest on banknotes other than by deflation.

In practice, though, no government really recommends zero inflation, and even less negative inflation, nor even an objective of total stability of price levels on the average term, which would imply that any period of inflation was balanced later on by a period of equivalent deflation. Which means, just as hypocrisy is the homage of vice to virtue, that the monetary authorities implicitly recognize that a little inflation must be a good thing for real activity.

There is no doubt, actually, that monetary policy affects economic activity and employment—because of the rigidity of prices. The thesis of the neutrality of money, or the impotence of monetary policy, supposes that all agents correctly forecast future inflation and, especially, that they immediately adapt to this forecast the price of the goods and services that they offer, including that of their labor. It is this absence of any inertia in the setting of prices, their perfect flexibility compared to the correctly forecast inflation, which strips currency of any power over growth and employment.

In the real world, however, prices are never perfectly flexible. They are slow to adjust and fairly "rigid"—if only because of the uncertainty which affects forecasts of inflation like all other forecasts. One has only to see the errors which are made each year and each quarter by the professional economists who spend all their to time trying to predict growth and inflation. Why would the average employee, or the average tradesman, do better than these qualified professionals?

Even if he were able, besides, he might not want to. In Europe, indeed, the rigidity of wages is reinforced by the vast apparatus of the welfare state, which lavishes social assistance, generous unemployment allowances, regulated minimum wages, and progressive tax on incomes, so many provisions that increase the relative advantage of the non-working population over the workers. Moreover, assistance to the enterprise, by deferring the prospect of bankruptcy and the reallocation of the factors of production that they employ, contributes to making employment permanent, which brings about further resistance to declining wages, and thus in the long term an increase in unemployment.

Together with wage rigidity, the general rigidity of prices causes similar reactions in the economy and makes the handling of the monetary policy effective. If the prices remain unchanged, an increase in the money supply creates quite real additional incomes and thus additional demand for goods and services, which stimulates production. Conversely, a reduction of the monetary supply destroys incomes and consequently decreases the effective demand for goods and services.

This is what Friedman stresses on multiple occasions in his *Monetary History of the United States,* when he ascribes several episodes of serious recession that have occurred in the United States, including the Great Depression of the Thirties, to the unduly restrictive monetary management of the Federal Reserve System.

If the prices and the wages are rigid, a monetary contraction will choke activity and will generate unemployment. Admittedly, in the long run, the prices and the wages will end up dropping sufficiently so that with unchanged monetary incomes, the consumers feel once again that they are rich enough to make purchases, and so the costs of the firms will have decreased in rather strong proportions so that it becomes profitable again to increase production. But this adjustment is likely to require a great deal of time. And in the interval the depression expands.

This means that the management of interest rates and exchange rates significantly affects growth, in particular if a recession comes on the heels of any shock independent of the macroeconomic policies such as, for example, the oil crises of the Seventies. One cannot count on a fast downward adjustment of wages to reduce companies' production costs and by this means to restart production and sales. A long wait and a high level of unemployment would be required in order for wages to be adjusted. In the interim, a policy of lowering interest rates and of monetary creation and lowering the exchange rate can remedy the decrease in demand and the rise in costs. In the Seventies this caused a strong acceleration of inflation, but made it possible to avoid a much more serious braking of economic activity. One can imagine what would have been the level of unemployment of the Seventies if the governments had put in action a sufficiently restrictive monetary policy to obtain zero inflation!

The effectiveness of currency creation in reviving an economy is, of course, contingent on the existence of outputs available to the firms, in terms of machinery as well as of workers. If all the equipment and all the employees are already 100% occupied, the printing of additional money will not be able to further stimulate production and will be reflected entirely in price hikes.

This explains why the Phillips Curve tightens toward the vertical when unemployment passes below its "natural" rate that corresponds to the institutional conditions of full employment. Beyond this point, monetary stimulation translates into more inflation and less and less effect on growth. One pays for the additional point of growth with higher and higher prices.

But on the other hand, a monetary policy can be excessively conservative, attacking growth too strongly and unnecessarily maintaining an unemployment rate higher than its structural level, to reduce inflation less and less effectively. Trying to bring it back to the vicinity of zero can entail a prohibitive cost in terms of increasing unemployment above its "natural" level.

On the Phillips Curve this last determines the rate of inflation which is compatible with "effective full employment." Seeking to reduce inflation below this level consequently will involve super-unemployment, a conditional unemployment which could have been avoided, and which produces only insignificant benefits in terms of disinflation; one pays more and more dearly, in terms of unemployment, for the additional point of disinflation. Financial conservatism becomes increasingly expensive.

The objective of zero inflation, according to the positioning of the short-term Phillips Curve, can be very far in the range of the rates of unemployment, far above the "structural" rate of equilibrium. That is what is happening today in the French economy where the rise of the prices is less than 1% per year and tightens toward zero, but where unemployment threatens to exceed 13%.

The conclusion is thus that it is advisable to establish the monetary policy in relation to the "optimal" rate of inflation (that which makes it possible to reduce unemployment to its long term incompressible or "natural" level), rather than to establish an arbitrary and inflexible inflation target, independent of its effects on unemployment, and which is likely to devastate the real economy.

Are Consumers and Companies Sensitive to Interest Rates?

In a closed economy, the definition of the monetary policy consists of the Central Bank setting short-term interest rates at its own discretion. In an open economy where the exchange rate plays an important role in determining imports and exports, and consequently the general level of activity, the parity of the currency (its external price) also contributes to establishing the monetary policy.

These are the reasons why the interest rate contribute to the definition of the exchange rate, through the influence that it exerts on the international influx and outflows of capital, i.e. supply and demand for the national currency. Raising the interest rate attracts international capital in search of a higher rate of return. Investors thus buy national investment instruments such as treasury bills or public and private debt. They must pay in francs and thus become buyers of francs and sellers of their own currencies. The franc's rate of exchange with respect to these other currencies goes up. The franc is appreciated. And conversely, when the Central Bank lowers its short-term interest rates, capital leaves France in the search of more remunerative investments, the francs are sold and other currencies are in demand. The franc is depreciated.

A restrictive monetary policy, which sets high short-term interest rates, at the same time, makes for a "strong" exchange. And conversely, if one wants to revalue the currency it is necessary to take into account the Central Bank's interest rates of intervention. The same holds true for "defending" a very high fixed parity of exchange or maintaining a constant exchange rate with respect to a foreign currency that has a tendency to be appreciated. That is the case of the Deutsche mark during the last few years, and especially since the reunification.

When the mark is appreciated compared to the dollar or the yen, the franc must be appreciated in the same proportion, and if the mark depreciates the franc must be depreciated also and in the same way. That means that the Bank of France must copy very closely the movement of the interest rate set by the Bundesbank if she wishes to maintain fixed parity with the mark; unless the Bundesbank adjusts its monetary rates on the French rates, or both, jointly decide how to adjust their rates. But that would require a common view as to what would be good monetary policy for each partner.

However, as we have seen, monetary, and thus exchange rate policy, significantly affects national economic activity. Thus it is necessary that the economic situations be exactly similar in two countries for the desirable monetary policy to be identical there.

Objections are often heard that interest rates have only negligible importance, for consumers as well as for producers. If that is true, why don't the banks double or triple their rates? Actually, a high interest rate which makes consumer credit more expensive dissuades, indeed, a certain number of consumers from making purchases on credit, and thus from buying at all. The consumer who is sensitive to a few centimes' difference on his usual daily newspaper obviously reacts to changes in rates that result in differences of several hundreds or thousands of francs gained or lost over several years.

In addition, a higher interest rate reduces the value represented by future incomes that the households anticipate, for example, that of stocks and investments. The owners of these assets are thus impoverished by this rate increase. Modern theory shows that the current level of consumption depends not only on the current incomes of the given period, but on the level of patrimony. When wealth increases, the households consume more, even if their current wages have not gone up. And the inverse is true when the value of the patrimony goes down.

A high rate also makes short-term business credit more expensive. It dissuades a certain number of companies from developing their activity and their investments, first because many firms, and especially the smallest, are financed mainly by bank credits in the short run, and then because the level of the short term rates act upon the long term rates which more directly affect the investments of the larger companies.

The Central Bank's increasing the rates of intervention, while limited to the financial market, thus affects by contagion every economic decision of consumption and investment. In this way it reduces the growth of production and, consequently, that of employment.

These domestic effects of interest rates are doubled by international effects in an open economy because of the connection between interest rates and the exchange rate. A fall in interest rates causes an outflow of capital as investors seek more substantial remunerations elsewhere. There follows a depreciation of the franc that affects the prices of all the French goods and services on the foreign markets, insofar as the interior tariffs in francs remained unchanged. Indeed, the French firms set these prices in francs according to their production costs and demand on the French market.

Following the fall of the franc the offerings of the French firms instantaneously become more competitive. Exports increase. French production increases. At the same time the foreign firms' prices, constant in local currencies, increase when they are converted into francs. Their offerings on the French market instantaneously become less competitive. French imports decrease. The consumers turn away from imports, to the benefit of French producers. The French firms' production is stimulated.

A depreciation of the franc thus lowers, on the international markets, the costs of the French firms, compared to those of foreign firms. Wages which were too high compared to those of the competing foreign firms are thus "lowered for export" by a depreciation of the franc, without the employees having to bear an immediate reduction in their income inside the hexagon of France. It is true, however, that they will have to pay dearly for imported products that they consume, but to some extent they can choose instead competitive French products.

An appreciation of the franc will produce the contrary effect, reducing French exports and increasing imports, which exerts a depressive effect on national production.

When the French enterprises complain about international competition from countries with lower wages, they do not understand in general that the essence of their difficulties comes from overvaluation of the franc caused by the "export premium" of the constant wages paid in France. It is not the wages of Sri Lanka that penalize our firms significantly on the world markets. It is above all the appreciation of the franc in the wake of the mark, as a result of the policy of financial fundamentalism.

In the long run, French firms will adjust their prices in francs to adapt to these new economic circumstances. But they will be impeded in this by the equilibrium of conditions in the French labor market. Employees will not accept an arbitrary reduction in their real wages for the pleasure of seeing the franc appreciated. And all the provisions of the welfare state will support them in their resistance. That is the underlying reason for which the monetary fundamentalists make the welfare state their principal target. Without driving down wages, no lasting policy of revaluation is possible, except by continuously increasing the level of unemployment, which has been the case since the beginning of the decade. Or by succeeding to increase the productivity of labor much faster than our competitors, which is not easy in a world of intense competition.

This means that the real effects of the variation of the exchange and the interest rates on economic activity are fundamental and at the heart of the current problems of the European economies. A systematic policy of appreciating the exchange tends to slow down growth and, if it is sufficiently strong, possibly can stop it completely.

If the short-term interest rates and the exchange rates did not influence companies' and households' levels of production and consumption, and thus the growth of the economies, it would be an indifferent matter to practice one monetary policy rather than another. And fixed exchange rates, even a single world currency, would be essential for reasons of convenience in trade. There would be no reason to have variations of the interest rates and the exchange rates as they only disturb and hinder trade in goods and services.

That is, articulately, the view of businesses, since they are focussed on the consequences of the variations of exchange rates which affect them directly, without studying what that rigidity costs the economy overall. This last aspect relates more to macroeconomic analysis, the study of the consequences public decisions impose on the overall level of activity and prices, which the firms tend to take as a given.

Business's point of view on the exchange rate policy is thus somewhat partial and therefore inexact. The relevant question to pose to them should relate to the combined consequences of the exchange rate and should be stated: "Do you prefer stability of the exchanges, even at a price of reduced growth, or flexibility of the exchanges accompanied by stronger growth?" That certainly would lead them to modulate their answer.

A single currency adopted by two countries is only the extreme case, irreversible in theory—or at least not easily reversible—of fixed exchange rates. In this situation only one monetary policy can exist, the same short-term interest rates and the same exchange rate with respect to the other currencies then being implemented by the economic agents of the two countries. The policy of the Deutsche mark standard, by anticipating the substitution of a single currency for the current national currencies, constitutes such an extreme case.

It imposes the policy of continuous disinflation on all Germany's partners, which is justified in Germany's case by the tensions of reunification, but is completely inappropriate for the other European economies that are suffering from under-activity, where unemployment largely exceeds its "natural" rate. The tendency toward revaluation of the mark, which results from the Bundesbank's anti-inflationary monetary policy, thus leads to exchange rates that are too strong for the currencies of those countries applying to merge with the euro. It is an exchange rate-induced recession that extends throughout Europe, with a disinflation that makes sense only for Germany.

Deflation and "Disinflation"

But does this analysis of disinflation's effects apply across the board? Is it valid for other countries and other periods? Can we verify that the monetary and exchange rate policy always exerts significant effects on the economy's real equilibrium? This should be the usual case apart from those periods, which are rare, when all the productive capacity is fully utilized.

Many episodes of contracting money supply, in various times and various countries, show that it is very generally accompanied by recessions of economic activity, either simple deceleration of the growth rate, or reductions in the absolute level of production for a few quarters.

It is especially the case in the United States, as Laurence Ball and Gregory Mankiw demonstrate[3], in quoting the Volcker experience of 1979. As Chairman of the Federal Reserve System (the United States' central banking system), Paul Volcker was more decisive than his predecessor, William Miller, in fighting strictly against inflation. From the time he arrived, in 1979, he decided to practice a policy of tight money, and it is easy to explain by this simple fact the deep recession that accompanied the disinflation that began in the Eighties. It was even baptized "the Volcker Recession," and rightly so.

In the same way, Christina and David Romer[4] have demonstrated, from the minutes of the Federal Reserve Board, that when the Open Market Committee, on seven occasions, decided to modify its monetary policy to reduce inflation, there followed in each case a lessening of production and a reduction of employment. These observations indicate not only that money is not neutral with regard to real activity, but more, that monetary contractions are a major source of the economic cycles in the United States.

Admittedly, one can support, as some do, the view that the causality is the other way around, and that the recessions determine a reduction in the demand for currency and thus a contraction of the money supply. But the precise historical narrative approach of Friedman and Schwartz, like that of Romer, make it possible to show that it is indeed monetary contraction which precedes the contraction of the economy and not the reverse.

It is thus, for example, that the passivity of the monetary authorities during the economic collapse of the Thirties is often ascribed, not to the development of the real economy that would have brought on a revival, but to the death of Benjamin Strong in October 1928. His successor having hesitated to practice an expansionist monetary policy, renounced it in favor of launching a severe monetary restraint intended to calm the feverish speculation on Wall Street—which may be said to have caused the crash in 1929—and then amplified the banking crisis and engendered, by contagion, a collapse of the real economy.

In the same way, recent economic works, in particular those of Laurence Ball of Johns Hopkins University, and also all the disinflation experiments of the Eighties show that restrictive monetary policies slow down growth and increase unemployment.

That was proven by the analysis of 65 case of policies of reduction of a moderate inflation implemented in the OECD countries since the beginning of the 1960's[5]. It comes out from this work that we have no example of an occasion where the reduction of inflation did not require a real sacrifice of growth and employment. Any reduction of the level of inflation contains a real economic cost in terms of lost growth and reduction of the possibilities of consumption.

All things considered, that means that the short-term Phillips Curve exists indeed, as mentioned by R. J. Gordon[6]. Those who set the economic policy thus cannot choose an arbitrary inflation rate without determining a rate of unemployment at the same time. Consequently, it is dangerous to set a goal for inflation as the only criterion of monetary management, without worrying about employment.

Conversely, the only conclusion of economic policy that the partisans of monetary conservatism want to draw from the existence of the inflation-unemployment trade off is that it is necessary to be doubly vigilant and to avoid any inflation since it entails an economic cost without bringing a lasting advantage. Thus it would be necessary to get out of it sooner or later, which will be costly in terms of reducing growth. Inflation would then have a double cost, initially in and of itself, but later because of the reduction of future growth that will be required to suppress it.

What is more, accepting a little inflation would have the effect of reducing the rate of unemployment below its "natural" level, which would cause inflationary tensions (an "overheating") in the economy, demand being pushed beyond what production can supply. This rise in inflation ends up becoming part of the anticipations of the economic agents, which moves the Phillips Curve upward. It is then necessary to seek a rate of inflation increasingly higher simply to maintain the rate of unemployment at its natural level. On the whole, well-being is reduced compared to the former situation, because of the real cost of inflation.

This is why it would be advisable to abolish any inflation purely and simply. The ideal would be zero inflation.

But this argument does not hold water either. As we suggested earlier, there is indeed an optimal inflation rate for a given economy, an inflation that corresponds to the "natural" rate of unemployment on the Phillips Curve. In sum, an "inflation of full employment." And there is no reason, theoretical or practical, for this inflation level to be zero.

Striving for zero inflation thus will generally place the economy below the level of inflation of full employment. That will push unemployment above its "natural" level. The economy will function then in "under-inflation" or in "relative deflation."

Indeed, nothing says that the position of the short-term Phillips Curve will be such that the inflation rate corresponding to "natural" unemployment will be at the zero level. That might happen, but it remains highly improbable. It would be a very special case indeed, for the rate of inflation corresponding to natural unemployment can take *a priori* any value according to the households' and the business's reactions to the creation of money. In other words, the level of inflation corresponding to full employment is indeterminate. It may be very different in different economies.

What is more, it evolves over time, since it is noted that the short term Phillips Curve moves. With the result that achieving full employment (at the natural rate of unemployment) supposes that one reaches a level of inflation which will change from time to time. And the inflation of full employment varies even more when one takes into account changes, over time, of the "natural" rate of unemployment.

The goal of a constant rate of inflation at an unspecified, arbitrary level, is moot and even harmful for growth and full employment. Even a positive inflation can be below the inflation of full employment and consequently, taken as criterion of good monetary policy, can lead to a recessionary situation. Thus, one should not set a goal of constant inflation if one wants growth with full employment, but should adapt the monetary policy both to the development of inflation and to that of employment, as do the most pragmatic and most reasonable central banks.

This is an essential and new conclusion to interject into the debate on monetary policy and the choice of an exchange rate policy. It is radically opposed to the European doctrine of monetary fundamentalism.

For a Positive Inflation

The choice of a target for price increases ranging between zero and two percent, maintained in France to preserve the parity with the mark, proves thus completely arbitrary compared to the needs of the economy. It chronically penalizes growth. The concept of a natural rate of inflation, on the contrary, condemns the principle of monetary union which establishes the management of the currency in adherence to a single inflation target aligned on that of the least inflationary countries, such as was defined at Maastricht.

Nonetheless, the governments and the central banks of many countries more and more often are using inflation targets to guide their monetary and financial policies. It is the new international dogma of monetary policy. It has been taken up in particular by the Bank of France and will be, tomorrow perhaps, by the European Central Bank if the single currency becomes a reality.

Such an objective is characterized by its permanence in time (for it is often registered explicitly in the statutes of the Central Bank) and its uniqueness in space. It supposes that the same rate of inflation is good in any period for a given national economy and that it is also good for all national economies. It is supposed to be universally valid, as well for Canada, New Zealand, Germany, France, Belgium, Greece and Spain as for Brazil or Argentina. Admittedly, for these the last two countries there will be some doubts and one will concede perhaps that specific political characteristics justify the impossibility there of obtaining inflation rates as moderate as in Switzerland or Germany. But the same rate will have to be implemented in just about every country in Western Europe in the event the single currency is realized.

On various sides, however, one wonders what would be a good policy for the central banks. Can they and must they follow simple and automatic rules to determine the interest rates and monetary growth, and if so, what would those be? These reflections hinge on the need for practicing a monetary policy that takes into account not only the objective of a single and fixed inflation rate, but also that of employment and economic growth.

Anyway, that is what the governments recognize implicitly when they tolerate inflation targets that vary slightly from one country to another. It could be due to a simple random choice. But the defenders of dogma will maintain, rather, that it is due to the pressure of certain groups that "prefer inflation" because it constitutes "an easy policy" which favors them; without any other explanation.

In this Manichean view, the governments represent reason and truth. The groups that demand a monetary policy that allows for growth are the ones that represent error and weakness. The choice of an inflation rate other than zero would then represent a concession to the irrationality of politics.

But a more profound reason for the dogmatists to make this concession of choosing an inflation rate other zero has to do with their implicit recognition of the insufficiency of the economic analysis upon which their conviction rests. In other words, they admit that the monetary policy and the rate of inflation do exert an effect on the real economy.

The rigidity of prices, which form the basis of this influence, was often denied by excellent economists who excluded it from their analyses because it seemed to them an inexplicable aberration. However, our knowledge evolves quickly and some recent works analyze convincingly the optimal behaviors that are generated by these frequently observed[7] rigidities. They result quite simply from the fact that price and tariff adjustments have a cost for companies as well as for consumers. With the result that everyone waits until it becomes really necessary to change the price, and the size of the change required is sufficient, before they have the nerve to do it.

It follows that, after a change in the market conditions, prices are adjusted only after some delay. This explanation of inertia, or imperfect flexibility, of prices and wages gives a rational basis for the existence of the Phillips Curve and for the effectiveness of monetary policy that many economists refused to accept since they could not connect it to rational economic behavior.

Through these behaviors of rational inertia and the relatively slow price adjustments that result from it, the shocks that constantly disturb the various markets will cause a rise in the general level of prices, which will move randomly over time. Thus a "natural" inflation, varying from period to period, results for each level of real activity. That explains movement and the instability of the short term Phillips Curve[8].

One can then deduce from these analyses that the "natural" or "optimal" rate of inflation, the notion of which I proposed above, will also move randomly according to the shocks which disturb the various markets.

The natural rate of inflation, or "full employment inflation," is then specific to each country and to each period because the shocks that disturb the markets are never precisely the same ones.

Before Milton Friedman proclaimed that inflation was "always and everywhere a monetary phenomenon," i.e. one that came up only on the heels of an increase in the supply of money circulating in an economy (which, by extension, allows us to suppose that only money supply can create inflation), many authors had stressed the existence of a form of inflation resulting, for example, from the rise in certain prices on certain markets: raw materials, labor, energy. In sum, they point to inflation "by costs." The weakness of this analysis lies in the fact that it would still require an increase in the monetary units in circulation for this inflation to become effective, "valid."

According to new analyses of the rigidity of prices, the prices of equilibrium change permanently on the various markets that make up an economy, because of the variations in demand, the growth of international competition, and technological advancements. But companies will change their tariffs only when the cost increases they experience exceed a certain magnitude, because it is expensive to change menus and catalogues. That requires efforts of reflection and judgement, and the use of expensive human and financial resources. It also disturbs the daily operation of the firm and the consumers' purchasing decisions. It is thus rational for the firm to accept this cost only when the price change is really important and necessary. The majority adjust their prices on average only every two or three years.

So if, for example, market shock comes from rising costs, the greatest ones will lead to increased tariffs, while the weaker cost increases will not be reflected in the business's selling prices. Consequently, the changes in the relative prices of equilibrium which act at every moment in every market will not leave the general price level unchanged. When major increases occur at the same time as a multitude of small declines, the general level of prices nevertheless will go up because only the first will be reflected, the firms not lowering their rates based on small cost reductions.

It follows that the adjustments of the relative prices in the economy will bring about, according to the statistical distribution of these changes, either the rise or the fall of the general level of the prices, i. e. of inflation. A typical example is the oil price hike in the Seventies, which caused at the same time a rise in prices across the board, before it was even supported by the creation of additional money.

That came only later on, to create an obstacle to the sharp increase in unemployment.

There can thus be an inflation that does not result from the creation of money. Its existence springs from the movements of relative prices together with the rigidity of the wage rates that the firms apply.

In this case, if the monetary policy is unchanged, the nominal money supply remaining constant, the goods and services, now more expensive on average, will fight for the means of payment which remain constant in quantity, which is equivalent to a reduction in the real money supply. The economic agents are impoverished and activity slows. The monetary policy, although constant in nominal terms, has become more restrictive in real terms.

The initial inflation target is therefore lower than the new rate of inflation of equilibrium of full employment. To go on in this way will cause under-inflation or a "relative deflation," that will push the economy toward recession and under-employment.

Under these conditions, continuing inflation that remains positive, but sub-optimal, may prove "relatively deflationary." A policy of positive inflation, which usually will be judged lax, can nevertheless push the economy toward recession.

The French economy thus chooses today a rate of inflation too low for its economic situation, which prohibits full employment, and it pays for this "under-inflation" or "relative deflation" through unjustified mass unemployment.

The central bankers' argument in favor of an inflation target fixed in time and identical for every country might be that the progressive integration of the economies will eventually bring closer the Phillips Curves of the Member States of a large market having the same currency. But nothing indicates that it has to be that way. On the contrary, according to the theory of international trade, the intensity of exchanges would have to accentuate the specialization of each member State in the monetary zone. And if the structures of activity of two economies remain different, the common shocks which affect their various markets will produce different inflationary results.

Moreover, each country's Phillips Curve will move in the course of time and nothing guarantees that its movements will lead to convergence.

Thus it is necessary to question the very idea of a convergence of inflation rates as well as the use of a constant inflation target as a guide to monetary policy. Nevertheless, these two ideas are at the heart of the plan to build the single currency.

SINGLE MARKET, MULTIPLE CURRENCIES

The reasons which were put forward, particularly on the occasion of the debates accompanying the fine-tuning of the 1990 Delors report, to justify the development of a European currency are primarily economic in nature. In a word, the integration of the national markets of the member States of the European Union, already largely realized, made it necessary for several national currencies to be turned into a single currency, in accordance with the slogan "Single Market, Single Currency."

The line of argument that flows from this watchword relates to the statement of the economic costs of the use of various currencies in transactions. A single currency, which would make it possible to reduce these transaction costs, would support the exchanges better. That is fairly incontestable. The question is how to assess the order of magnitude of these potential savings and how they compare to the costs generated by the single currency.

Fallacious Arguments In Favor of the Single Currency

The supposed costs of using multiple currencies are diverse.

Initially, exchange brokers encumber the transactions between agents from various countries, and they proliferate in a continental space where the tariff barriers have been removed.

In the second place, there are costs related to uncertainty about exchange rates. To protect themselves from these exchange rate risks, and only partially, buyers and sellers must obtain insurance policies, which are expensive. Without that, the existence of the risk could lead them to reduce the volume of their exchanges, whereas the creation of the common market was intended to increase them. The Commission calculated these costs on average as 0.5% of the yearly national product of each Member State.

In addition, significant fluctuation of the exchange rates would affect export and import firms seriously and for long periods, to the extent of driving some out of business through bankruptcy, without any economic justification.

The new currency would also make it possible, according to a third argument, to fight inflation more effectively. The independence of the central banks, in conformity with the fundamentalist doctrine, seems to be the only lasting rampart against a return of inflation. The European Central Bank, whose statutes are copied after those of Bundesbank, could be proof of the same determination as the latter in prolonging the stability of prices, which is supposed to benefit growth and employment, at least in the medium and long terms.

Lastly, a single currency for Europe would represent a significant international force, because of the size of the European countries' foreign trade. It naturally would be very much in demand and would make it possible to attract the whole world's capital, which would support financial industries on the continent, and "would thus give us a global role," especially in the international financial institutions such as the IMF and the World Bank but also on the markets. Europe could then "speak as an equal to equals with the United States and Japan."

All these supposed advantages call for a careful examination from the simple economic point of view, an examination at the end of which they appear singularly over-estimated by the promoters of the monetary union.

Let us mention right from the start that the interest in fixed exchange rates does not seem to be as universal as the Europeans, or at least the French, suggest. The United States and Japan do not practice fixed exchange rates with regard to Europe, nor between themselves. And neither does Germany with the non-European countries. That does not prevent these countries' firms from developing their export activities and their technology, and from doing it rather well.

Theoretical and empirical studies have shown that actually the fluctuations of exchange rates do not seem to have affected much the firms that operate in international trade. Indeed, these fluctuations operate erratically but stay at a roughly stable level, or follow a regular pattern which, since they can be anticipated by the economic operators, is incorporated into their calculations of price and profitability. This central tendency, defined by the "parity of purchasing powers," i.e. the equivalence of exchange which equalizes the price of the same good on the various national markets, constitutes a reminder. Currencies that diverge from that parity return more or less quickly, generally in the space of three to four years. A depreciation will be followed later on by erratic fluctuations in the direction of appreciation, with the result that over a longer period the profits and losses on transactions on foreign currency tend to balance each other out.

However, the value of firms is not determined over a three or four-year horizon but over a period much longer, as modern financial studies have shown. It follows that if companies are affected by the fluctuations of exchange, it is rare that they could endanger their very existence.

More especially as contemporary firms, during this time of globalization, have diversified the destination of their exports and the source of their imports. And this tendency increases over time. It should not be imagined that foreign trade will polarize more and more, inside the great commercial areas such as Europe, for example. International trade is more and more also intercontinental trade. This means that business's exchange rate risks are diversified and compensate one another.

A firm that exports a large proportion of its production to only one market is extremely vulnerable to the exchange rate variations between its national currency and that of its destination market. But if the same firm exports the same production to ten markets, its exchange rate risk is greatly reduced because the bilateral parities will not all move in the same direction. Just as a portfolio of shares well-diversified is less risky than a portfolio invested on only one bond, in the same way a firm which has a well-diversified portfolio of international customers will see its exchange rate risk reduced to almost nothing.

Lastly, many European exporting firms are more concerned with the developments of the exchange rate of the dollar compared to their national currency more than with the intra-European exchange rates. International trade is largely dollar-based and many European exports are destined for countries located outside the Community. In this case, the problem of the instability of exchanges will remain, even if the single currency is implemented. A European firm's exchange rate risk with the yen and the dollar will not disappear with the creation of the euro.

It follows that the argument of the cost of protecting companies against exchange rate risks falls apart. The same applies, at least partially, for that of reducing the volatility of the external markets, and this for a large percentage of European exports. Continued protection

from the yen risk and the dollar risk will still be needed, and undoubtedly also against fluctuations of those European currencies which
would not be allowed to form part of the inner core of the single currency (since it appears today far from probable that many other countries will be ready to merge with the Deutsche mark between now and
1999).

The question, then, is whether intra-European trade concerning
only the countries of the monetary hard core will grow faster, and will
represent a greater value, than trade between European countries that
are not part of the core--and more quickly than the trade between
European countries of the hard core and third countries outside the
Community. Given the already very large extent of internal trade relations within Europe, proliferating for many years, one can safely bet
that it is the ties with third countries that will grow most quickly in the
future. And in this case, European monetary union will not bring a
substantial solution to the problem of the fluctuations of exchange
rates.

Does the fight against inflation constitute a stronger argument? By
no means. European countries, and the others besides, made a success
of their disinflation in the Eighties by following national monetary
policies independently from each other. And this in spite of the lam-
entations of the macroeconomists who wished coordinated policies,
the advantage of which, moreover, was never decisively proven in
spite of superabundant literature that waxed lyrical over the virtues of
the G7. The various governments thus showed in practice that inflation can be reduced unilaterally, which signifies that monetary policies
preserve their effectiveness even in an open international economy
where goods and capital are very mobile.

Some of the countries that reduced inflation had independent central banks. Others, conversely, preserved a conservative system of

subordinating the central bank to the political authority. There are some indications tending to show that, in average terms, independent central banks obtain levels of inflation lower than those of central banks under governmental control. But the difference in result is not very large. And nothing proves that a European central bank would be better on the matter than national central banks whose independence would be guaranteed in the same way.

Besides, that is what concerns the German financial milieu, and more particularly Bundesbank, with regard to the construction of a single currency. And this is why Germany requires such precise commitments to the rigid rules of what must be in the future the European monetary policy, by excluding any reference in particular to employment or to growth targets, and by claiming and imposing additional and superfluous unnecessarily restrictive budgetary safety constraints.

What, then, are the supposed advantages of this single currency? First of all, savings in the costs of trade, but that is not very significant if competition between the financial banks and industrial establishments plays to the full. Currently, the high costs of exchange transactions rather concern the tourists, whose currency exchanges constitute only a minor part of the ensemble of international transactions, much smaller than that of the other sectors of the economy.

And for this, are we supposed to pump up the "hot air" of the euro and risk getting entangled in the institution of a federal administrative layer?

There remains only a very vague, but obsessive, argument on the advantages of the "economic power" of a "great" international currency. But nobody ever defines precisely what would be the hypothetical advantages of this "very great currency."

It is true that the international use of a currency depends to a large extent on the international trade volume, and particularly on the exports, of the country which manages it. From this point of view, a single currency used by all the European exporters would play a more important role than the current mark, and *a fortiori* than the franc.

But the direction of causality goes from the importance of the national economy to the importance of the currency, and not the reverse. Certainly, one may have a currency that is fairly widely used at the international level, even if one is a small country, like Switzerland. But nobody claims that Switzerland benefits from specific economic power owing to the fact that its currency is used as a refuge by international investors.

Conversely, there certainly exists a possible advantage to the local financial institutions of having a currency whose use is widespread in the world. Money is the raw material of financial firms. They collect margins on its use. And one can imagine that the national financial institutions earn more than their foreign competitors on transactions carried out in their own currency.

But the financial institutions' interest is only that of one sector of the economy. It does not equate with the interests of the whole country. If a hard currency, widely used in the world, is good for the banks' current accounts, it may be unfavorable for those of the automobile and chemical producers, even for the agro-alimentary industries. A hard currency may entail considerable drawbacks. International demand for the currency can cause appreciation, as has been felt in Germany for several years or, repeatedly, in Switzerland. That makes business more difficult for exporting firms and slows down economic growth; it even contributes to the complete destruction of certain industrial sectors. At a time when the world banking industry has surplus production capacity and its economic profitability has become doubtful, it is not at all clear that it is good policy to sacrifice other sectors for the good of the banking sector.

There is indeed a "burden on economies of a reserve currency." England felt its effects when the pound sterling was the first international currency. It is also the reason for which the United States gave up playing an explicit role as manager of a reserve currency in 1971 by abolishing the link with gold and allowing the exchange rate to fluctuate in a policy of benign neglect.

All things considered, for a country or a continent, to have a reserve currency is more of a banker's dream than an advantageous deal for industrialists, exporters, or finally for consumers. There are indeed limits to the increases in productivity that the firms can achieve in order to deal with a chronic revaluation of the exchange rates.

It becomes clear that the promoters of the single currency were financial and banking officials rather than industrialists or exporters. Could it be that their perspectives were too narrowly corporatist?

Common Markets are not Necessarily Optimal Monetary Zones

But along with the illusory advantages of the single currency it is necessary to take account of the reality of the permanent cost that it will undoubtedly inflict on the countries that adopt it.

Above, we saw that the fixity of the exchange rate, which imposes an identical monetary policy on two national economies, is likely to cause sub-optimal inflation in one or the other, or in both. Then it compromises full employment in the economies concerned. Monetarist policies thus defend all their interests vis-à-vis achieving full employment, even in an economy that is very open internationally, for which the rate of exchange plays a decisive role in determining the level of production. This conclusion goes radically against monetary orthodoxy, which maintains that the management of money supply becomes less effective the more open the economy is to the outside.

For two economies to fix their exchange rate permanently, which corresponds in the extreme case to establishing a single currency, would thus require that the "natural" rate of inflation is the same in each. That is one of the conditions that must be met in order for a fixed exchange rate between two countries to be advantageous.

But contrary to what the dogma of monetary conservatism would have us believe, which only considers the rate of inflation into account when drawing up economic policies, the convergence of inflation rates is not the only economic condition that should be met if a fixed exchange is to be implemented—or its extreme alternative, the creation of a common currency. There are others, quite as important.

It is particularly interesting to observe that these conditions are not met for the European countries overall. The latter thus do not constitute, among themselves, a single, "natural" or "optimal" monetary zone.

In this case instituting a single currency (or a simple system of rigidly fixed exchange rates) between countries that do not naturally or structurally constitute an optimal monetary zone causes losses of production and growth compared to the economy's potential. It prohibits full employment of the factors of production, including labor.

The majority of the countries of Europe having characteristics which do not make them members of a "natural" monetary zone, the constitution of a single currency will cause recurring delays of growth there and will consequently lower the standard of living compared to what it could be under a flexible exchange regime and independent monetary policies.

Indeed, beside the most limited, or even illusory, advantages, monetary unification entails costs that have not, until now, been adequately studied. The theory, however, has existed for a long time. The theory covers the conditions which must be met in order for several countries to derive advantage from participation in the same "monetary zone," a theory known as "optimal monetary zones." It shows that a currency common to several countries is advantageous only when their economic structures show certain well-defined characteristics. Otherwise, the level of wellbeing will deteriorate in the participating countries.

This analysis thus runs contrary to the slogan "Single Market, Single Currency," which implies that all the countries having decided to practice thoroughly free trade among themselves should benefit from abandoning their monetary autonomy.

Let us quickly point out the characteristics which make it advantageous to use a common currency, then the consequences which this creation involves for the countries which do not have these characteristics and thus do not form part of an optimal monetary zone.

In the simplest case, that of two countries, it is easy to demonstrate that the fixity of the exchange rate, and thus its extreme version, the creation of a common currency which excludes by definition any later adjustment in the rate, is the most desirable if the two countries' principal foreign trade is massively directed toward each other rather than toward third countries, if the flows of labor, goods and capital is greater between them than with the outside, if the structures of production are similar there, if the usual rates of inflation are similar, and if the sizes of the economies are different, one being smaller than the other. Which means, in principle, that the two economies actually make up only one economic entity, the smaller being only an appendage of the larger.

Indeed, an economy very open externally will be penalized more by the instability of the exchange rates if a large proportion of its consumption and its exports will be subject to significant price variations which will upset producers' and consumers' calculations alike. This will be all the more true if the economy is small and thus its domestic prices will tend to be adjusted according to the international prices, rather than the reverse.

For the same reason, an economy that carries out the bulk of its exchanges with one principal partner will obviously have an interest to stabilize its prices in trade with this partner who definitively affects its activities. On the contrary, a country whose foreign trade is geographically very diversified will depend relatively little on its exchanges with any one of its many partners. An exchange rate adjustment with one of them could be compensated by possible adjustments in the reverse direction with others. In that case it is less important to fix the exchange rates, since the exchange rate risks compensate each other.

We already examined in detail the reasons that make it desirable to have similar inflation rates, effective but also "natural," between economies wanting to adopt fixed exchanges or a single currency. But until now, in the conception that has become traditional of an inflation rate arbitrarily chosen by the monetary authorities, only political good-will, in itself unexplained, could lead to a divergence of the rates of inflation.

The necessary convergence of inflation, in a fixed system of exchange, thus rests finally on similar preferences on the part of the governments or central banks. On the other hand, in the concept of a "natural" rate of inflation, the behaviors of optimization of the economic agents as regards fixing the prices must be similar and the economies considered must be liable to identical shocks. That brings us back to the question of similar structures of production as a condition for success, as stated by the theory of optimal monetary zones.

Finally, a strong mobility of the factors of production, labor and capital, also facilitates the fixing of the exchange rates because it constitutes a good shock absorbing mechanism for the random shocks which affect the local economy. If an economy taking part in an area of fixed exchange rates undergoes a recession alone, it can adapt insofar as its workers and its capital emigrate temporarily toward the other regions or countries in the area, in which the activity is more constant. The first can then do without the stimulant of a depreciation of exchange to support its activity and the use of local factors.

It is possible that two economies having all these characteristics except the convergence of inflation may be led to adopt a fixed exchange rate. For example, two economies which have different rates of natural inflation but a very concentrated mutual trade, strong mobility of the factors of production and a pronounced international openness, can have an interest in fixing their exchange rate, all these factors compensating for the differentials of inflation.

It is also possible to compensate for the absence of some of the other conditions necessary to an optimal monetary zone through public interventions, in particular transfers of incomes between the expanding areas and the areas in recession. A single monetary policy which does not make it possible to prime the pump in the area in recession could be maintained if the taxpayers of the expanding area contribute to a central State tax payments which may be used for helping the unemployed of the area affected by the crisis. That is what happens in the United States, in particular, which does not truly constitute an optimal monetary zone although it has had a single currency for a long time.

Several Dollars for the United States?

The States of the North-American Union have rather different environments of economic activity. From this standpoint they do not meet all the conditions of an optimal monetary zone even though the mobility of the factors of production is high there. The effective rates of inflation differ among the states while their "external" trade is not necessarily concentrated on the neighboring States.

According to a study by the Boston Federal Reserve Bank, five or six large areas constitute optimal monetary zones within the United States. The U.S., because of this, does not fulfill the economic criteria that justify the use of a "single dollar." Several different types of dollars could be used in the American Federation without notable excess cost.

To prove it, the author of the article, Geoffrey Tootell, takes the example of the oil crisis of 1974. It is a perfect case of "asymmetrical shock" in that certain States are exclusively oil importers, and big users, while others use somewhat less, and some, like Texas, are major producers. Following the quadrupling of the price of oil, the wealth of Texas suddenly shot up, the price of its crude exports to the other States having been multiplied instantaneously, whereas the price of its imports remained unchanged.

Conversely, Michigan, a big producer of cars and for this reason very sensitive to variations in the price of gasoline, was considerably impoverished overnight. Afterward, the growth rate of real income per capita reached 1% in Texas while it fell to –6% in Michigan.

Since prices and wages are not perfectly flexible, neither when falling nor when rising, unemployment increased in Michigan and was reduced in Texas. In the absence of an independent monetary policy in these two states, the real wages had to drop in the first and go up in the second, or the fired workers in Michigan would have had to move to Texas to find employment opportunities there which were also increasing.

But in reality the wages were rigid and the mobility of the employees insufficient, which means the imbalances persisted. A differentiated monetary policy would have made it possible to slow down the economic overheating in Texas and to stimulate activity in Michigan, abolishing the shortage of labor and wage inflation in the former (as well as the resultant inflation of local prices) and reducing the underemployment and recession in the latter. Such an independent monetary policy would have resulted in a variation of the rate of exchange between the "Texan dollar" and the "Michigan dollar," if it had been possible. It also would have restored the balance of payments in each State, promoting exports from Michigan and developing imports into Texas.

Tootell emphasizes that even in the event of wage flexibility and geographical mobility of workers, it is enough that the governments have different preferences regarding inflation growth for each one of them to have an interest to preserve its monetary independence.

These different preferences seem proven among the large industrialized countries, as shown by the example of the divergences of the economic performances following the oil crisis of 1973. From this date to the end of 1975, the United States accepted an increase in inflation of 2.9% and 3.6% for unemployment, while Great Britain accepted an inflation increase of more than 15% but only 1.4% in unemployment. France let its prices go up by 4.8% and its unemployment only by 1.3 percent (like Great Britain, choosing inflation rather than unemployment), while Germany on the contrary caused a 1% drop in its inflation at the cost of a 2.7% increase of its unemployment.

Let us add that these preferences can be understood better if they are not discretionary or completely arbitrary but reflect differences in structural costs under the conditions of the arbitrage between inflation and unemployment from one country to another. The elected political officials only translate into prices and employment rates the economic characteristics of the countries that they represent.

Continuing his reasoning, the author undertakes to show that the United States does not constitute an optimal monetary zone. Indeed, the economic ups and downs are very little coordinated between most states. Consequently, there would be an advantage in periodically adjusting the rates of exchange between "regional dollars," if they existed, within the United States, because of the relative rigidity of wages, the imperfect mobility of labor, and the asymmetrical shocks that affect these states.

In fact, judging from the disparities in the regional economic situations, it seems that there are several optimal monetary zones within the Union. The Far West is one (California, Oregon), the Southeast another, then the agricultural states of the "Farm Belt" (Northwestern), the Midwest industrial states, the southeastern Atlantic States, and New England. It is interesting, too, to note that the division of the Federal Reserve System into eleven banking districts corresponds fairly closely to these optimal zones.

Other economists have arrived at the same conclusion, using different techniques. With regard to the United States, the authors show that the various states are associated in several optimal monetary zones, which differ according to whether one acknowledges a larger or smaller number of such zones inside the Union. If one considers there are five of them, for example, then California, Colorado, Hawaii, Maine, North Dakota, Utah and the State of Washington form one area, while Michigan on its own constitutes a separate monetary zone. The authors also calculate the (substantial) loss of well-being resulting from only one currency—or even two or three—being imposed on all the states of the Union. They show that with twenty to thirty currencies, the fifty American states would see the losses of well-being that result from sharing one currency among themselves drop to almost nothing.

However, although not being an optimal monetary zone, the United States was able to preserve just one currency for more than a century. If they were able to do it without too much damage to their economy, it is because they benefited from compensatory mechanisms of tax redistribution.

But is this example relevant for Europe?

Let us note first of all that the process of monetary centralization occurred there only slowly and rather late in the game. The Federal Reserve System, the central bank of central banks, was established only on the eve of the First World War, that is to say more than a century after the Union was founded. That shows certain prudence on the part of the fiscal authorities and at the same time indicates the probable difficulty of the task of unification.

In addition, as we noted above, it is true that a single monetary policy can be implemented in a nonoptimal monetary zone provided that a system of income transfer applies the tax receipts from the growth areas to assist the areas in recession. The federal tax system takes care of that in the United States, as observed by such recognized economists as Martin Feldstein[11], Xavier Sala-i-Martin and Jeffrey Sachs.[12]

That is what allows a system of fixed exchange rates to be maintained within one country, whereas, at the international level, the system of the Gold Standard and later that of Bretton Woods burst under the pressure of disparate economic situations in the member states.

The quasi-automatic transfers induced by the federal tax are used to some extent as insurance for the member states by redistributing the revenues from the prosperous states toward the states that are less favored by the economic situation, through the mechanism of federal social assistance programs. Since the income tax scale is progressive, the redistributive effect is increased.

Sala-i-Martin and Sachs calculate the magnitude of this effect. They find that on average, for a dollar of lost income, an American state sees the tax levy decreasing from approximately 33 to 35 cents, while the federal transfers that it receives increase by a value ranging between 2 and 5 cents, around an average of 3 cents. On the whole, the income after taxation for a state in recession drops only by about 62 cents on average for any dollar of production lost; that makes the differential (or "asymmetrical") shocks more bearable for each state of the Union.

Due to this process, it becomes less essential to preserve an independent monetary policy and the accompanying adjustable rates of exchange. It follows that economists are inclined to conclude that the existence of a common tax system, constituting a kind of insurance against asymmetrical shocks in the economy, makes it possible to maintain an irrevocably fixed exchange rate between several states that do not constitute an optimal monetary zone together.

As Sachs and Sala-i-Martin write:

> . . . It is a lesson which the partisans of a European single currency must contemplate: the creation of a unified currency without a provision for federal insurance (an implied "tax") could very well lead this plan to complete failure.

Admittedly, we have on our continent a tax levy at the European level, but its size is negligible. According to the authors' calculations, a recession of a dollar in one of the EEC countries will decrease that country's European tax levy on average only by one half a cent, compared to 34 cents in the United States.

The conclusion that emerges from this analysis is that monetary union is impossible in the absence of a preliminary political federation, with a fully equipped tax apparatus.

It could nevertheless happen that the conditions of an optimal monetary zone would be fulfilled in practice between certain European countries, making it useless, or at least less necessary, to create a European State and to establish a federal continental tax system.

We will examine the empirical question a little further. But first, it is important to stress what would be the consequences of a currency union among states not naturally forming an optimal monetary zone.

Under these conditions, fixed but occasionally revisable parities constitute a minor evil. One can adjust the external price of goods and services like that of labor relatively frequently, while retaining the internal rigidities.

But immutable parities, like those that the monetary zones represent, are dangerous if the economic conditions diverge between member states, which will surely happen sooner or later. Then the only possible means of correction is through the failure or the creation of firms; and meanwhile through transfers conducted by public finances.

Several experiments with fixed exchange rates have proven these shortcomings. In particular that of the Thirties, when several European countries, after the adventures of the war, attempted to return to the pre-War parities while re-establishing the system of the Gold Standard that was given up during the hostilities.

But it is also what we are experiencing in the Nineties with the experiment in the course of the Deutsche mark standard. And it is, finally, what the African countries of the franc zone tried at the end of the Eighties.

The Economic Drama of the Thirties

The system of the Gold Standard, which implied fixed equivalen-
cies of exchange rates among the participating countries, was restored
after the world war as a sign of returning to "healthy" currency management after the inflationary excesses required by the conflict. Taking into account the parities retained at the time, and of the scarcity of
gold, this decision contributed decisively to the deflation which was to
transform, between 1929 and 1931, a serious but non-catastrophic
stock exchange crisis into a financial landslide—and then into a major
depression. Recent works by macroeconomists and currency historians like Barry Eichengreen and Jeffrey Sachs[13] establish this fact and
reinforce Friedman's analysis of the monetary policy's responsibilities
in the economic drama of the Thirties.

Because of the depth of the crisis, Great Britain was first, among
the countries that had chosen to return to the former system, to signal
its abandonment of the gold standard in 1931. However, as of December, 1929, Argentina and Uruguay had suspended the gold regulation
while Hungary, Paraguay and Brazil were unable to maintain the parity of their currency. In 1930, the exchange rates of Chile, Vene-
zuela, Peru, Australia and New Zealand fell.

The international difficulties were followed, in Europe and America, by financial crises: a banking crisis in the United States at the end
of 1930, in Austria and Germany the following summer. When Great
Britain was forced to devalue its currency, several other countries did
so as well, although they were not really constrained to do so. At the
end of October, 1931, all the British dominions (except for South Africa), the rest of the British Empire, the four Scandinavian countries,
Portugal, Egypt, Bolivia and Latvia depreciated their currencies.
They were followed in six months by Japan, Greece, Siam and Peru.

A new cycle of depreciation started with the fall of the dollar in

1933. In March, Roosevelt had introduced restrictions on the movements of gold and currencies . . . The following month he made it illegal for private individuals to own gold. At this point, the dollar
started to float. By raising the dollar price of gold, on several occasions, the Roosevelt administration carried out a substantial devaluation. That caused a series of retaliatory or "competitive" devaluations.
South Africa joined the sterling zone in fluctuating. The currencies of
Latin America continued to fall. The yen, by falling, broke its quasi-
fixed tie to the sterling zone. The only great currencies that remained
freely convertible were that of the gold bloc: France, Belgium, Hol-
land, Italy, Poland and Switzerland. In March 1935, confronted with
increasing difficulties since the country was open to the outside, Belgium had to give up the gold bloc. It was followed by the other countries of the Bloc in 1936.

The effects on industrial production were immediate. The countries
that did not depreciate their currency, or that depreciated only by a
little, saw their 1935 production fall or stagnate compared to its 1929
level. That was the case for France, the Netherlands, Italy and Germany. Those, on the other hand, that depreciated their currency by
30, 40 or 50% relative to 1929 increased production by 10, 20 or 30%
compared to the same year. That was the case for Great Britain, for
Sweden, Denmark and Finland.

The same thing happened in terms of exports. France, in this area
as well, paid a high price for its "monetary health." And the consequences were exactly the same in the arena of investment, which remained stagnant. Monetary orthodoxy reduced investment in France,
Belgium, Italy and Germany, whereas it was kept up in the Scandinavian countries and in Great Britain.

Incidentally, the strong currencies caused increasing real wages
while at the same time unemployment reached catastrophic levels,
whereas the countries that chose the way of depreciation saw only
moderate increases in the real level of pay.

Countries that devaluated could adopt a more expansive monetary policy and lower the discount rates of their central banks, which encouraged a general fall in rates and increased at the same time the incentive to invest.

On the whole, the effects of the currency depreciation appeared massive and positive. Were they, as has long been maintained, detrimental to the countries that maintained parity with gold? Did the downward fluctuation constitute a *"beggar-my-neighbor"* policy, an aggressively competitive policy of devaluation that consisted of robbing Peter to pay Paul?

Eichengreen and Sachs do not find empirical evidence of this, because the effect of reviving the devaluationist economies actually benefited the non-devaluationist countries by supporting global economic activity.

Finally, the last holdouts of the gold standard threw in the towel in 1935-1936, after having sustained considerable economic damage, and to no purpose. The experiment of returning to excessively fixed exchange rates and parities, i.e. blind monetary conservatism, was carried out at a huge cost to France, Italy and Germany, and not only in economic terms.

The Mistake of the Nineties

The same kind of scenario occurred again, incredibly, at the beginning of the Nineties. In 1992-1993, during the collapse of the ECU under the attacks of the international operators, several European countries chose a policy of returning to fluctuation. Italy, Portugal, Spain, Sweden and Great Britain did not, strictly speaking, devaluate their currencies—for devaluation comes into play only in a system of fixed exchange rates where one goes from one managed parity to another. But they chose to let their currencies float relative to the mark and also relative to the currencies of the countries which decided to remain aligned on it, that is France, Belgium, the Netherlands, Austria and Switzerland. In fact, this second group of countries decided to pursue a policy of revaluation in the medium term while the Deutsche mark tended to be appreciated vis-à-vis all the other national currencies.

We thus have new laboratory experiment on the consequences of the choice of a conservative exchange policy. We can compare the performance of the countries which let their currency float against the very different performance of the countries which chose to follow the mark in its rise.

Such a study was recently conducted by Robert J. Gordon, who measured the results of the two groups of nations over the period from the second quarter of 1992 to the second quarter of 1995, the last date for which the necessary macroeconomic data were available[14].

The average revaluation of the five countries' currency tied to the mark was 10.2% over the period, while the average depreciation of Italy's, Portugal's, Spain's, Sweden's and Great Britain's reached 22.2 percent. Both groups experienced an acceleration of the growth of the nominal national product, but real growth was definitely higher in the countries that depreciated their currency—2.7% over four years against 1% for the countries which let their currency appreciate. And inflation decreased in the two groups, which completely contradicts the dark forecasts of uncontrolled landslide that the partisans of the euro formulated with regard to the countries that would give up fixed parity with the Deutsche mark.

The evidence is thus noted: flotation does not necessarily involve continuous depreciation of the exchange rate nor explosive domestic inflation. A phenomenon even more surprising for the fundamentalist thesis, the countries that chose to fluctuate downward have in fact recorded a disinflation more marked than the re-evaluationist countries! Minus 1% of inflation over the period against only minus 0.6% for the countries that remained in fact in the mark zone!

The nations that chose to float thus gained all the advantages: stronger real growth and speedier disinflation than those of the countries of the mark zone, in total contradiction to the euro-monetarists' dogma.

This enlightening experiment confirms what we saw previously: the exchange rate remains an important and effective instrument of macroeconomic policy. An adjustment of the parity can appreciably diminish the development of real growth and employment.

In addition, the experiment also shows that the contemporary international environment precludes a fast recovery from inflation, except through an outrageous policy of issuing money, and that national monetary policies must take this into account and find ways to profit from it.

Because of the weakness of its inflation, France in particular has significant room for maneuver to revitalize its economy. It would have been logical, and advantageous from this point of view, to readjust the franc's value compared to the mark since 1991 or 1992. But it is not still too late to do it, a few years later, contrary to what the euro-monetarists illogically maintain. On the contrary, the need is felt all the more strongly insofar as the countries of the small mark zone have, in fact, continuously revalued their currencies during the period, while those of the group of countries that opted for floating allowed theirs to be depreciated. It follows that the first group, and France particularly, have a rate of unemployment today higher than the "natural" rate, the majority of specialists estimating that this latter must currently be in a bracket ranging between 7 and 8% of the labor force[15].

While the example of the "devaluationist" countries (or, more exactly, those who chose the downward fluctuation), shows that one can dispense with fixed exchange rates without giving rise to inflation, we must necessarily conclude that monetary and exchange policy is responsible, together with the budget policy, and without the benefit of price stability, for at least four points of unemployment in France, or approximately one million unemployed.

Africa — Victim of the Strong Franc

The experiences of the franc zone all lead in the same direction. Created more than a half-century ago, the franc zone, which combines the principal French-speaking countries of Western and equatorial Africa as well as the Comoros, ensures the convertibility of the CFA franc and the Comorien franc with the French franc at a fixed parity. This has remained unchanged since 1948 and 1979 respectively, at the rate of 50 CFA francs and 50 Comoriens francs for a French franc. That has led all the countries concerned to follow the development of the French franc and that of French inflation.

During the years when the French franc was periodically depreciated and when inflation in France was at the average or higher than the average of its trading partners, that hardly posed a problem for the African countries. The franc's exchange rate did not penalize their exports and the rate of French inflation was sufficient to facilitate the adjustments of internal prices without fear of recession.

But things changed during the Eighties, and the danger of fixed parities between countries that do not form part of an optimal monetary zone was revealed in all its magnitude.[16]

Indeed, since 1985, the global economic situation of all the member States of the area deteriorated badly, a continuation in particular of the side effects of two major external shocks.

Initially, these countries underwent a decline of almost 50% of their terms of trade between 1985 and 1993, because of the considerable and prolonged fall in world prices of their principal exports, especially cocoa, coffee, cotton and oil. If one wished to avoid too sharp a contraction of the export earnings, these developments called for a decrease in the exchange rate, which would act quickly on the price of exports without requiring a painful internal deflation which always takes time.

In the second place, this loss of competitiveness was aggravated since 1985 by the strong appreciation of the French franc with respect to the currencies of the principal partners and commercial competitors of the zone. In addition, the whole zone was handicapped by various structural and sectoral problems, in particular the relatively high wage costs.

Admittedly, the fall in global demand, the "internal adjustment," would have made it possible to cause a drop in the price and wage level, but would have led to a recession. That was tried initially, as parity with the French franc seemed a taboo, in particular given the attitude of the French authorities who saw the African countries' difficulties as the result of too lax a budgetary and monetary control, whereas to a great extent they resulted from the two shocks just mentioned.

Thus, in spite of the efforts at internal adjustment, the economic and financial situation continued to degrade and the per capita income continued to decrease. The public sector, in particular, had to deal with mounting problems. The State deficit grew deeper because of the contracting of the tax base, attributable mainly to the export sector's loss of competitiveness and the substitution of various products for the imports, and to the development of the black market, including illegal imports. The rise in production costs, particularly wages, contributed to a strong decline in public firms' profitability and led to a reduction of their tax contributions while requiring increasingly massive budgetary aid.

In such a context, the attraction of the franc zone for investors was greatly decreased—in spite of the stability of the prices and of the exchange rates—and capital flight accelerated considerably. Several countries tried to respond to these difficulties by intensifying their internal adjustment. However, the extent of the shocks and the scope of the imbalances were such that these measures, although necessary, were not sufficient to restore economic activity.

The pursuit of this strategy was balanced by an increase in taxation on the productive sectors and by disheartening cutbacks in certain expenditures for public administration and priority equipment (health, education, infrastructure) which compromised the chances of a lasting return to growth and private investment, and which also testifies to the comparison of the principal economic and financial indicators of the zone and the other sub-Saharan countries since the middle of the Eighties.

Thus between 1986 and 1993 the average growth of real GDP of the countries of the zone reached only 0.1% a year, whereas it was 2.5% in the African countries that were not part of it[17]. During the same period, the budget deficit was hovering at 7.6% of the GDP in the zone, against 5.6% for the non-member countries.

Finally, after having denied the evidence for a long time, and facing the threat of having the zone burst apart, France accepted the diagnosis of overvaluation of exchange. On January 11, 1994, in Dakar, the member states decided on a new strategy encompassing a realignment of the parities of the CFA franc and the Comoro franc: a drop of 50% in foreign exchange for the first and 33% for the second.

The monetary realignment as well as the accompanying measures on budgetary, monetary, wage, structural and social matters led to a very significant improvement in competitiveness of the economies concerned, and re-established the overall economic equilibrium. Global growth soon found a positive rate, ranging thereafter between 4 and 6% in real terms. This strategy created a surplus that made it possible to reduce the public sector's net requirements and to eliminate the domestic and external arrears.

This radical and successful experiment shows to what extent prices, and above all the price of the national currency (the rate of exchange), play an essential part in the development of the real economy. In the face of growing imbalances in the economies of the African countries, the French leaders' initial reaction was to blame the laxity of the African budgetary and monetary control, maintaining that in no event must they devalue the CFA franc, for fear of encouraging this supposed lack of rigor. In the same way, typically, the African leadership often reacted by wondering what made foreign investors "stop playing their part" and refusing to invest in their countries and to take "normal" business risks.

Actually, neither of these two phenomena was particularly liable for the decline of the situation: they were only the outcomes. The fundamental responsibility lay in the rigid fixing of the exchange parity in circumstances that called for flexible adjustments. The role of prices, that economists always emphasize, was thus thrown into sharp relief.

And it is exactly the same phenomenon (although less acute this time) that is hitting European countries today and particularly France. Rigidly fixed exchange rates, with a currency that tends toward revaluation, i.e. the mark, are choking exports, strangling economic activity, and slowing growth, which destroys the equilibrium between public finances and social budgets. In such a context, the good souls who do not recognize the role of prices or who do not want to question the political taboo of the exchange parity with Germany, generate a profusion of diagnoses on the need for increased rigor, for a sober reduction in public spending, for greater flexibility in the labor market (read: a reduction of monetary wages even before the prices come down in a similar fashion) and other "adjustment," i.e. deflationary, policies, which can only further reduce activity, further unbalance the public accounts, and add to unemployment.

The lesson of the franc zone should be studied better by our political leaders, including the ultimate consequences which it just missed causing—its own disappearance, pure and simple.

The Calculus of the Monetary Union

The simplest structural determinant indicating that a common monetary policy can be appropriate to several countries is the parallelism of the economic conditions. If it is strong, each country will require an expansionist policy or a contracting policy at the same time.

A first approach to weighing the desirability of a monetary union would thus be to measure the correlation of the cycles of economic activity in the various countries under consideration. A strong correlation or a strong convergence of the economic situations leads one to think that there are few really asymmetrical shocks, or that these shocks, when they occur, only slightly affect the economies of the zone under consideration. Then it would appear possible to give up national monetary independence without loss.[18]

Observation of the combined economic situations, in recent years, shows that the European economies are hardly in sync in their development. The convergence of the economic situations remains weak. It appears that the convergence that does exist traces the border of an optimal monetary zone in Europe around Germany and the small countries close by (the Benelux countries, the Netherlands) to which one might, to a lesser extent, add France.

A more precise approach consists in studying the relationship between the monetary regimens chosen by the various countries of the world and the characteristics that, according to an analysis of optimal monetary zones, should lead them to incline either toward fixed exchange rates, or toward flexible exchange rates—such as the concentration of foreign trade, the mobility of the factors of production, the openness of the economy and the distance between trading partners.[19]

Indeed, a systematic relationship can be detected between these national characteristics and the choices the countries make between fixed exchanges and flexible exchange rates. Simply applying this general relationship to the European countries, taking as a reference point the exchange regime that it is convenient to adopt with regard to Germany, immediately shows us which of them would have an interest to maintain fixed exchange rates with the Federal Republic and which others have an interest to preserve floating exchanges.

According to these calculations, it is in the interests of Germany, France, the United Kingdom, and to a lesser extent perhaps Italy, to preserve floating exchanges.[20]

On the other hand, it is clearly in the interests of Denmark, Belgium and the Netherlands to enter into a system of fixed exchange rates with Germany since their theoretical index of the optimal exchange regime is negative.

It is striking to note that this conclusion roughly confirms the cogency of the existence of the small mark zone, which joins together precisely those countries most convinced of the need for the euro.[21]

All that is strictly in conformity with the theory of optimal monetary zones, which indicates that small countries having intense and concentrated exchanges with a large neighbor have an interest in fixing their exchange rate vis-à-vis its currency. Such, indeed, is the case of Belgium, the Netherlands, and Austria, which in fact already belong to an informal mark zone.

It appears, on the whole, rather less recommended for France, Italy, Great Britain and Spain to link themselves by a common currency with Germany.

But the extraordinary thing about the situation is that, for its own part, Germany should not have any inclination to choose fixed exchange rates. The exchange indicators, calculated in relation to all the other European countries, indicate that it should opt for floating. All things considered, Germany does not have an interest in the construction of a mark zone in Europe!

Is this a paradox? Not really. Of course the issue is Germany's own economic interest. Furthermore, the economic actors are quite conscious of these underlying realities, even if they do not analyze them rigorously. Thus German public opinion, for various reasons, is opposed to the euro by two against one, thus matching the results of economic calculation.

It has been observed clearly in recent years that it would be best for the German economy to go it alone in monetary matters, without inviting other countries to share in defining its policy. The Bundesbank has rigidly maintained its fundamentalist monetary policy without any concern for its partners, leaving them to take the trouble of coming into alignment with the mark to whatever degree they wished—but without modulating its trajectory in order to help them. On the contrary it has, on two occasions at least, moved to force out of the European system of fixed exchanges certain currencies that were endeavoring to approach the future euro without the directors of BUBA really wishing it: the pound sterling, and the lira.

From this point of view, the official attitude of France is contrary to its economic interest since all its governments have militated in favor of the euro. That can only be explained by a non-economic, that is, a political motivation. As in the Thirties, it is again for reasons largely historical, political and philosophical rather than purely economic that certain countries remained pegged to the Gold Standard while circumstances pointed to its abandonment. [22]

And finally, that is what our monetary officials explain to us when they state that they want monetary union in order to create a political union, to keep Germany in the bosom of the Western European nations, against the temptation of going it alone and then leaning toward the center and the east of Europe.

The policy of monetary union thus constitutes a fundamental economic misinterpretation for its two principal protagonists. If one insisted, in spite of everything, on cloaking the heterogeneous unit represented by the Franco-German couple in a single currency, one would have to accept the creation of a federal political entity whose common budget would replace that of the member states. As nothing of the sort is conceivable by the time the euro is due, the pursuit of monetary construction is sure to generate recurring economic and exchange crises, the prospect of which actually makes the implementation of the single currency rather unlikely.

If it were to be implemented overnight through a discretionary political act, the European Monetary Union would lead to explosive asymmetrical shocks of economic and social difficulties in some of the member states in the "non-optimal" monetary zone.

And the difficulties may be growing. Unification of a large market indeed leads to increasing industrial specialization within the component economies. However, specialization makes national economic structures diverge. It follows that the shocks, which periodically have affected such and such sector, will become increasingly specific to one nation or another with the development of the single currency due to the single market.

This tendency toward specialization across national economies may be observed in the form of North-South polarization by which one area is impoverished while another prospers. The same effect will accentuate the disparities within the European space, in spite of costly transfers of regional assistance from Brussels. The latter will be no more able to attenuate the local differences than Milan was able to solve the problem of the Mezzogiorno, nor for that matter, than Bonn or later Berlin, could prevent the destruction of the industry of the eastern Länder, victim of German monetary unification.

Monetary integration is thus a double-edged sword. Contrary to the Commission's slogan, the single market actually calls for increased differentiation of monetary policies instead of a single currency.

The adage, economically founded and not conceived from the simplistic administrative point of view, should have been: "Single Market, Multiple Currencies."

THE EURO IS NOT VIABLE

Under these conditions, the euro appears neither desirable nor viable. The stagnation in Europe, which particularly strikes those countries most engaged in the construction of the single currency, testifies to that.

If we put an end to the restrictive monetary policies that align the European currencies on the Deutsche mark, we could indeed re-establish competitiveness on the international stage (which would promote exports), and return to lower interest rates (which would stop the strangulation of production and consumption). A national monetary policy that regained its autonomy would make it possible for the economy to quickly return to growth like that which occurred in Italy and Great Britain after 1992.

By contrast, forcing heterogeneous economies to run while in the yoke of a single monetary policy necessarily provokes conflicts between the national governments. And that is what we see during the phase of convergence. But it will continue if the euro is established.

It follows that, instead of creating stability and confidence, monetary unification will cause monetary uncertainty and political conflict.

The phenomenon is not new. Several attempts at monetary unions between sovereign countries took place in the last century and at the beginning of this one. They have all ended up, after a few years, with the disintegration of these non-optimal monetary zones. It is a fate that prefigures that of the euro if its creation is carried out to the full term.

As the day of reckoning approaches, there are real problems that can no longer be ignored. How will the future euro be managed? Will it be the continuation of the mark, or a currency of compromise allowing an intermediate European inflation between that of France and that of Italy? And who will be on the list of countries accepted into the Founding Club on the first day of January, of the last year of the century? Will the euro space be truncated or expanded?

A Truncated Euro?

This is what seems to be taking shape in the deal-making that is going on around what will be the fate of all the Convention countries which, apparently, are completely outside the process of convergence. Perhaps France would wish only to join with the *de facto* mark zone that exists between Germany, the Benelux countries and Austria, but remain outside of the Maastricht process. That would require spelling out who would be able to vote and to manage the common monetary policy of this monetary mini-union.

Some people say this approach would preserve the future of the single currency, which other European countries would join with later on, even though they are not ready to take that step today. The advantages of this approach are scant.

In the first place, a single currency is more advantageous, when it is advantageous at all, if it can fix the exchange rates between a great number of trading partners. By fixing the exchange rate of the franc only with Germany and the Benelux countries, France's accession to the mark zone would protect us from none of the fluctuations of the other European currencies, which would preserve substantial margins of variation although differing from one country to another. In any event it would leave undiminished the problems of fluctuation of other currencies which are important for our economy, like the yen and the dollar.

In the second place, the idea which had prevailed in France when the idea of monetary unification was proposed, was that the French government was to take part, with the help of the other European governments, in jointly managing a clearly defined monetary policy. Instead, it now looks as though we would have to follow, without any power to influence it, a monetary policy that was unilaterally decided by the Bundesbank, according only to German interests.

Finding itself the only large country that was integrating itself institutionally with the mark zone, France could not rely on any other country to help influence the Bundesbank's policy. The "small monetary Europe" would then be reduced to France unilaterally giving up its monetary power to the benefit of Germany, without visible compensation.

The gravity of the economic and social consequences of such an act, elaborated above, should dissuade our leaders. It is permissible to make a mistake, but when the time comes, one must recognize reality for what it is and eventually change the policy. Current public debate and public opinion makes us think that these realities are more and more widely recognized.

A Weak Euro?

There is another possibility, which seems quite as probable. In the summer of 1997, indeed, the mark's and the franc's decline on the exchange market strengthened the dollar, which leads one to think that speculators anticipate a weak euro, just as German investors shift toward the Swiss franc and toward the greenback.

However, what dominates is uncertainty. The entry of Italy into the Founding Club, from the very start of the euro, if it were to be created as scheduled in December 1998, could also mean a strong euro. The European Central Bank would have to demonstrate that it is quite as capable of rigorous management as the Bundesbank. Besides, the more inclusive the Founding Club, especially with regard to countries whose fiscal virtue is relatively recent, the more guarantees of preserving monetary policy the Bundesbank would require.

The outcome depends mainly on the relation of the political forces involved. Furthermore, it calls for an explicitly political solution, insofar as the positions of various countries would be in conflict, due to the fact that the countries in question do not form an optimal monetary zone together. That is to say that optimal monetary management for one is not optimal for the other, and thus the political relations of force between states must decide on the single policy which will be implemented. But this prospect contradicts the Treaty's provision for being managed purely technically, without government interference, a provision that the Bundesbank defends tooth and nail.

These major conflicts and the uncertainties that they generate are, to tell the truth, not specific to the European Union. They inevitably occur every time one wants to control sovereign states via supranational monetary rule. The recent example of ex-Yugoslavia illustrates the same thing, as reported by Joze Mencinger, its former Economic Minister.[23]

Taking his place among the minority of eurosceptics, Mencinger hopes that the euro will not be created, not because he is opposed to the union of Europe but on the contrary because he favors it. According to him, the monetary union will definitively destroy the idea of European unification within just a few years. It is indeed surprising that this extremely important plan depends primarily on only one man, Chancellor Kohl, and on timeframes and rules that the European political leaders themselves may have set but in which they really do not believe. Isn't it surprising that the Maastricht criteria are articulated around price stability, which is not a current problem in Europe, and ignore unemployment, which has been the major burden in the last ten years and will continue as such for at least another ten years?

With the euro launched, the common monetary policy will deepen the rift between the member states, while unemployment and intolerance will preclude the free market of labor, which is an essential condition for viability of a monetary zone in the absence of massive federal redistribution.

In that case, the time is not far off when each one will feel exploited by all, as the former minister puts it. That was exactly the case of the late Yugoslavia. The parallel between the old dinar and the euro may appear absurd, but the resemblances between the two currencies are numerous. There is no more trust between the leadership of the countries who must together manage the future European currency than there was between the leaders of the ex-Yugoslav Republics, and there are no more common European values than there was "fraternity and unity" in ex-Yugoslavia (whose motto that was). A Sicilian differs from a Swede as much as a Macedonian from a Slovene. And if Yugoslavia died economically in 1990, it is above all because of the conflict over the dinar and the monetary policy that was being pursued.

For Mencinger, the introduction of the euro very much resembles the period before the independence of Slovenia, when the leaders thought they could separate monetary independence from political sovereignty. This turned out to be impossible. He concludes with these words: "I believe that monetary union without political union will be no more viable for the European Union than it was for ex-Yugoslavia."

The Final Disintegration of Non-Optimal Monetary Zones

Sovereign states do not share their currency. Several experiments with monetary union in Europe since the middle of the 19th century are recalled in an enthralling work by the director of the historical section of Nederlandsche Bank of Amsterdam, Wim F.V. Vanthoor.[24] Some of them turned out to be long-lasting, others collapsed after a few years. Thus it is particularly interesting, in the year of a great decision, to distinguish the factors of success and the causes of failure.

The author answers the question very clearly by distinguishing those monetary unions which accompanied the creation of new states that incorporated older and smaller political unties, from those which only corresponded to agreements on economic cooperation between states that retained their sovereign rights.

In the first category we find three examples: the political unification of the Swiss Confederation in 1848, the foundation of the German Reich in 1871, and the Italian unification of 1861. In each of these cases, new currencies were created which still exist today: the Swiss franc, the Deutsche mark, and the lira.

The second category includes the Austro-German monetary union that existed from 1857 to 1867, the Latin monetary union founded in 1865 and grouping Belgium, France, Italy and Switzerland more or less up to the First World War only to be effectively dissolved in 1926, as well as the Scandinavian monetary union, created in 1872, which also lasted until the Great War and went on, then, after a fashion, until the disappearance of the Gold Standard in 1931.

Political Preconditions

It would be facile to observe that only the monetary unions resting on a preliminary political union succeeded, while those that corresponded only to coalitions or alliances of independent states failed to survive the risks and shocks of international economic and political life.

At the simple level of economic reasoning, this is hardly surprising. On the one hand, indeed, since currency is, in the modern world, an instrument of financing and a bond of national debt, a currency common to several sovereign states can only cause serious political conflicts between them, insofar as their interests must, from one moment to another, diverge. In addition, economic theory and the experience of companies as well as countries teach us that alliances, when they are not imposed by a single state political will, in other words a monopoly of power, are intrinsically unstable. One may remember, for example, what happened with the oil cartel which made the industrial nations tremble in the Seventies.

The very existence of an alliance encourages each of its members to play his own game, contrary to the collective advantage of the ensemble, in a "lone ranger" or "stowaway" strategy, seeking to benefit from the discipline of paying passengers to travel freely at their expense. It is this fear that makes today's German leaders seek to make those countries wishing to take part in the common currency adventure pay a sacrifice similar to theirs in terms of rigorous and constraining budgetary control.

The author shows, with detail and precision, that an indispensable condition of the successful monetary unions was the preliminary political union of the states or principalities concerned (in fact within federal or confederate structures in the case of Switzerland and Italy), or the adherence to a certain regional autonomy within the German Empire.

The case of Germany, however, seems to contradict the need for a preliminary political union. One indeed observes a tendency toward monetary union since the establishment of the common market of that time, the Zollverein, in 1834, well before the political union of 1871. But this union in fact is limited to the introduction of fixed exchange rates in 1838 between the Prussian Thaler, circulating in the North, and the Gulden which circulated in the southern states, and favoring the already dominating role that the Prussian currency enjoyed within the German territories. This scenario approximates the current attempt to extend the "small mark zone" (the Benelux countries, the Netherlands and Austria) to France.

However, it was not until December 4, 1871, a few months after the foundation of Reich, that a true single currency was instituted, in the form of the Reichsgoldwährung, the most widely used coin, of which the mark was one tenth and constituted the unit of counting.

So it remains true that the creation of durable shared currencies was posterior with the creation of integrated states. Political union precedes monetary union.

To this interesting historical report by Vanthoor let us add some economic considerations on the differences between the context of the 19th century and our end of the 20th which, in our opinion, allowed for monetary unions in the last century but makes such enterprises improbable today. The creation of common currencies was supported, at the time, by two basic tendencies which one does not find today, or which, worse still, are reversed.

The first had to do with the international tendency to use gold as the exclusive basis of money circulating in every nation, which to some extent removed these currencies from political manipulation by the governments. Price flexibility, freedom of international movement of input factors (capital and labor), the fatalistic social acceptance of recessions as facts of life independent of the will of the public powers, made it possible to accept living without the economic shock absorber constituted by the variable exchange rate.

However, in spite of these favorable circumstances, the Austro-German attempts at union, the Latin monetary union and the Scandinavian union, which had been helped by the existence of this common "meta-State" reference to the value of gold, were doomed to fail either because of permanent political conflicts between the partner states, in the first instance, or to the military conflicts of the First World War and the disappearance of the international system tied to gold, for the two others.

The second condition, well illustrated by Vanthoor, has to do with the political integration of the partner states, a necessary and essential precondition to creating a single currency. Political disintegration and the exacerbated nationalism of the Thirties and Forties coincide with the disappearance of these fragile unions, leaving in place only the currencies of the integrated states.

In the same way, one may consider that the introduction of a system of fixed exchanges after the Second World War represents a variation of the German experiment of the years 1834-1871, before the foundation of the Empire. The politico-economic domination of one state over its neighbors can be used as substitute for integration. And in fact, the United States which, in 1945, represented about half the world GNP, founded a quasi-single currency similar to the ECU, built upon the gold standard, that is, the dollar standard, as Prussia had built a Thaler standard.

Thus, the economic asymmetry of 1945 led all independent countries, of very small size compared to the American giant, to define their currency in relation to hers. That conforms, by the way, with the theory of optimal monetary zones, one of the conditions of which is the asymmetry of sizes between partner countries. Moreover, the omnipresent exchange controls and the low mobility of capital, at least until the early Sixties, made it possible to defend fixed national rates of exchange.

But Western economies developed more quickly, catching up with the conditions of production and the standard of living of the most advanced country (the United States) and calling into question this asymmetry so that, with the liberalization of exchanges, the Bretton Woods system blew sky high at the beginning of the Seventies.

Thus, we can explain the contemporary period in economic terms, the same way Vanthoor describes the historical trends in Europe between 1850 and the present.

Chapter III

THE FALLACY OF THE
VERY GREAT STATE

There will be no durable single currency without a single European state, either federal or confederate. The euro is expressly conceived to cause the creation of such a continent-wide state. According to the federalists' strategy, the single market leads to a single currency and the single currency will call in turn for the formation of a single state. Setting up the single currency would thus lead necessarily to the construction of the European state they wish for.

In the preceding chapter we showed that the weak point in this reasoning is the assertion that the single market requires a single currency. The common market supports economic growth through the free development of exchanges, even when several national currencies coexist as, incidentally, the various experiments of free trade demonstrate, all over the world. But a uniform monetary policy applied to heterogeneous national economies inevitably penalizes some of them. Such a single policy thus appears to be inferior, as a means of producing wealth, to the differentiated monetary policies that adapt more precisely to the national needs.

A line of reasoning analogous to that which makes decentralized management, for a state or for a firm, appear preferable to the choice of a single and centralized hierarchy, uniform and rigid, leads to the conclusion that "custom made" monetary policies are better than a monetary policy common to several states. It follows that the single market gives better economic results with several national currencies than with a single one.

It is quite true, on the other hand, that the single currency calls for a single state. To such a degree that the attempts to construct common currencies for several sovereign states in Europe, attempted on several occasions since the middle of the 19th century, all fell through after fairly short periods. If one really wants a single currency in Europe it will thus be necessary to proceed urgently toward merging the existing states into a continental Super State, the "Very Great State."

But apart from its possible role as manager of the single currency, would it offer any kind of benefits to the European economies? Would it render any services that the current national states are not able to provide? And could these additional services justify the cost to national economies corresponding to the new taxes that it would be necessary to raise? Creating an additional layer of bureaucracy will appear legitimate only if it can prove its superiority over the current organization that enables several independent states to coexist within the European space. And a non-legitimate state has little future prospects in democratic societies.

In the field of commercial enterprises, the merger of several independent firms can seem advantageous insofar as it creates a "national champion" more able to compete on the international markets. But often this advantage exists only on paper, in the ministries. One single large firm is not necessarily more effective than several small ones. Only under very precise economic conditions is that the case. And the disappointing destiny of the industrial policy of national champions demonstrates clearly how superficial is this view.

The same applies to states. Creating a "super state" by merging existing national states is not necessarily a winning strategy, if it increases the operating costs of the bureaucratic superstructure. A state whose great size makes it ineffective and too expensive for the advantages that it provides, is a burden for the nation's production of wealth. A society's "overhead," when it is too high, penalizes companies and employees vis-à-vis international competitors.

At a time when organizations the world over are seeking to reduce their size in order to be more efficient, the super state that Europe wants to build seems a kind of paradox. The additional services that it is supposed to provide seem illusory. And the reduction of the national public expenditure that it is supposed to facilitate has only little chance of happening.

TOWARD THE SINGLE STATE

From the very beginning of the formation of a unified Europe, when the Economic Community was launched by the Treaty signed in Rome on March 25, 1957, a statist lobby has seen the creation of a common market as nothing less than a process that would one day be fully realized in the formation of a continental federal state along the lines of the American model.

Minorities within every nation, the federalist friends of Jean Monnet obstinately sought the institutional mechanism that could automatically and necessarily lead the signatory countries of the economic union to a political union that would forge the most powerful state in the world, even ahead of the United States; and presenting the peoples of Europe, *a priori* non-consenting, with an accomplished fact.

The reasons that inspire the federalists are various. For many, it is a question of making any future war between European nations impossible, once they are joined together within the same state. Others wish to have an impact on the world's destiny by giving back to these nations the leading role, which they had collectively held until the beginning of the century, marked since then by American and Soviet domination. For still others, it is essential to build the largest democratic state on the planet, taking as a starting point an ancient culture and a political model different from that of the United States. For some, finally, it is only logical to prolong a secular movement toward enlarging the size of the nation, such as had occurred in French history for example, and more recently in Germany, a trend which seems to them part of the natural order of politics and history.

The automatic passage from economic union to political integration appeared plausible in the first analysis: wasn't this the way that had led, in the last century, from Zollverein to Reich? The ambitions of the leadership elites, on both sides of the Rhine, echoed history in these terms.

In France, the economic and financial leaders traditionally have been obsessed by the regime of fixed exchange rates and the constitution of a great monetary zone which would give the franc an importance that it did not have, to the great irritation of our banker technocrats. This obsession resulted in the attempts of the Latin Union at the end of the 19th century, and the Gold Bloc after the First World War. Nostalgia for a global regime of fixed exchange rates became stronger after the disappearance of the Bretton Woods system in 1971. When the dollar declined to play an active part as the currency of reference, backed by gold, the way seemed clear for French initiatives for rebuilding the international monetary system on other bases, starting with Europe.

Political Origins

From this dual set of interests, federalist European on one side, French reconstitution of the international monetary system on the basis of fixed exchange rates on the other, a political plan was born for using currency to build a common market throughout a continental state. It provided for equipping the large market with a system of convergence of exchange rates that would evolve gradually toward a single currency. This in turn would generate the need for the construction a single state.

And that is indeed the stated sequence, acknowledged in part by the Emerson report, "Single Market, Single Currency," written at the request of the Brussels Commission then chaired by Jacques Delors. The end of the slogan, implicitly understood, was "Single Currency, Single State." But this last part of the program was to be made public only later on, as circumstances unfolded.

The plan was not new. It was originally put in place in France on the initiative of Valéry Giscard d'Estaing, in 1979, with the launching of the European monetary system. Insofar as it defined fixed but periodically adjustable exchanges, as in the Bretton Woods system, the EMU was viable, for it did not contain true rigidity of exchange rates or durable parities. But the second stage of the process, approached under François Mitterrand's second term in office, at the time of the Treaty of Maastricht in 1991, was much more formidable. It provided for definitively fixing the exchange rates, presaging the passage to a single currency that would be managed by an independent central bank on the model of the Bundesbank.

Circumstances had suddenly become more favorable for applying in practice the French technocrats' international monetary ambition.

At the end of the Eighties, the disappearance of the Soviet Union and Communism opened the way all at once for the reunification of Germany, which overnight stopped seeming like a remote dream and became an immediate possibility, which Chancellor Kohl seized. However, in a Europe co-piloted jointly with France, it would be out of the question for Bonn to carry out such a merger without the agreement of Paris.

The condition set by François Mitterrand, somewhat outgunned by a powerful and potentially dangerous partner, echoed the strategy he had adopted earlier with regard to his allies, and rivals, the Communists: to link himself closely with the adversary in order to better control it. Thus he asked Germany, as the price for France's assent to German reunification, to dissolve the mark into a single currency which a European super-Bundesbank would manage. The monetary eurofusion would later on lead to the political integration of the two countries and Germany would be definitively bound, made incapable of causing harm.

Chancellor Kohl, on his side, was ambitious to obtain a major role on the international political scene for his country, the first-ranking economic power of the continent. He accepted the step insofar as the new currency would be only a pure and simple continuation of the Deutsche mark and managed as such. Which, if worst came to worst, would be acceptable to the cautious opinion of German citizens and to the reticent Bundesbank.

Entrusting the management of a common monetary policy to an independent organization copied on the BUBA (Bundesbank) had, moreover, the decisive advantage of starting the two countries on the way toward political union but without requiring, in the immediate future, the establishment of a single political power. This avoided the dilemma presented by the impossibility of moving ahead by openly proposing, for democratic ratification by the people, the creation of a European federal state—a proposal that had no chance of being accepted.

At the same time, a model of monetary management was proposed to Germany that closely resembled its own. Indeed, the power of the Bundesbank would be enhanced by a partial dismembering of the economic power of the federal government, a solution that America had favored in 1949. Why not adapt the same formula to a Europe that by definition did not have, and could not have in the foreseeable future, any centralized and strong political power?

This form of political integration would have frightened the public and would have been rejected, as the plan for a European Community of Defense had been in its day, if it had been proposed openly and frankly to the voters from the start. All things considered, the chosen solution made it possible to preserve the plan. On the other hand, a European central bank holding the reality of monetary power under the, incidentally, poorly defined control of the Council of Ministers of the Member states, would constitute a temporary substitute for a European government, which appeared sufficient for the immediate task.

At the same time, monetarist technocrats would replace the elected political leaders. But it made the deal all the more feasible, that under the considerable inflation of the Seventies, monetarist doctrines had been disseminated throughout the political milieus and among central banking management. "Automatic" management of currency was recommended, barring governments from discretionary interventions and advocating the use of only "technical" criteria, such as a steady growth of the money supply, or pursuit of a stable inflation target close to zero. The specific conditions of the Eighties thus led to the separation of the monetary policy from the sphere of governmental responsibilities.

This solution appeals to the socialist President of France all the more so given that it corresponds to the traditional ambitions of financial technocracy and it allows, as a bonus, to carry out a convergence of the center Left and Right, while dividing the Right deeply for the long term. The UDF and the centrists indeed share with the Socialists the ambition to create a single European state. Their agreement on a common monetary policy leading to this goal gives rise to the "republic of the centers," that bipartisan consensus of the Eighties which constituted the source of politically correct thinking ("la pensée unique").

That doctrine, statist and European, is responsible for the most serious error of political and economic strategy of second half of this century.

Indeed, the plan to create a continental state using the lever of currency, inspired by the expansion of the Western states in the 19th and 20th century, would be revealed as anachronistic and contrary to the economic conditions that prevail at the end of the millennium. A continental state is economically ineffective today, goes against the tide of all organizational trends, will be superfluous for defending the interests of the European people and, moreover, will paralyze the essential structural reform which is the key to the continent's future prosperity.

Meanwhile, in the present, the disadvantages of monetary construction become manifest as it evolves. Fixing the exchange rates produces its noxious effects on the national economies by slowing down activity, by exacerbating imbalances of public finances and by pushing the level of unemployment higher and higher.

These difficulties cannot be denied any more, in spite of official propaganda, and the economists are starting to ask questions publicly. The plan's promoters are giving up on their sales pitch that was exclusively focused on the economic benefits of the single currency, no longer very credible, to fall back on presenting and defending the plan on a more frankly political basis.

At the same time they initiate a divorce from public opinion, which feels directly in its standard of living the disadvantages of the policy of convergence toward the euro. But the successive governments, their eyes very much on the imposing vision of the Very Great State, are sublimely oblivious to these minor vicissitudes. After all, it's only econmics!

For Reasons of State

The argument in favor of the euro was mainly economic at the start. The common market was supposed to call for a single currency which, making national prices immediately comparable, would enhance competition and would complete the market's unity. The single currency was thus considered essential to the full unification of the continental market. It would reduce to nothing the exchange rate risk and the brokerage costs for transactions involving the movement of men and goods between nations.

Without a convincing answer to the concrete difficulties of the convergence phase or to the economic arguments that show the major costs of constructing the euro, the federalists gradually fell back on the argument of the primacy of politics. Who cares what are the costs to the economy when one is concentrating on the important task of creating the indispensable European State? Only that project could guarantee peace in Europe and the world by no longer leaving the monopoly of safety in the hands of the United States, the *de facto* global policeman. Only that could defend the legitimate economic interests of France and its continental neighbors vis-à-vis the commercial "realpolitik" of America. And what better answer than the Super State, to oppose the invading threat of global markets, which in fact the French leaders continue to see as the disguise of the unbearable hegemony of the "Anglo-Saxon" and Japanese speculators?

In a world which is not really global but where the cooperative competition of regional commercial areas and "economic war," in other words protectionism, reign we need a powerful state—that is, of continental scale.

The reunification of Germany, which makes one fear both its return toward its natural Central European tropism and a renewal of nationalism corresponding to its increased size, then becomes the justification of every effort to politically link the Federal Republic to the French Republic in an indissoluble way. That is an ideal argument for those who always dreamed of building a European federal state on the model of the United States.

This plan was exposed, directly and completely, by the governor of the Bundesbank during the crucial time of 1991 to 1993, Helmut

Schlesinger. In an article entitled "Currency is only the Beginning," published by the weekly magazine *The Economist* (September 21, 1996), he perfectly summarizes the euro-federalist doctrines.

It is not difficult for a university economist, wrote Schlesinger, to find arguments against the single currency. Already, the European monetary system in place functions more or less as one currency, while nevertheless leaving the national governments with some macro-economic room for maneuver. What more will the single currency give us? And can we consider that the European Union constitutes an optimal monetary zone? Won't the monetary union create more problems than it can solve? Can it contribute to reducing unemployment? And who can guarantee that the countries that had recourse to inflation in the past will not do so again there in the future?

All these questions were examined during the preparation of the Treaty of Maastricht, continues Schlesinger. And it is necessary to understand that the monetary union is beyond economic argumentation and must be understood primarily as a political plan, like the European Union itself. And we should recall the German debates in the early Fifties, before the creation of the European Economic Community. To Chancellor Konrad Adenauer, who, like France, favored a Europe of six, they opposed his Economics Minister Ludwig Erhard, who pre-ferred a Europe of sixteen, conceived solely as a vast free trade area.

The majority of German economists, Schlesinger notes, were on the side of Erhard. And they were wary of French plans. But, he concludes, Adenauer's strategy, resting mainly on political considera-tions, carried the day and was, somewhat after the fact, a double suc-cess: the EEC constituted a remarkable center of attraction and today counts fifteen members, while Erhard's market policy today is very generally accepted in all the Convention countries.

This demonstration is however curious, for one may consider that it is actually Erhard who was right. He had seen very clearly that the real possibilities were limited as well as carrying inevitable risks for

Europe. At the horizon of the new century, the European Union of today, which is on the verge of extending itself to Central and Eastern European countries, is above all just a vast free trade area matched, it is true, as Erhard feared, with an ambitious and interventionist bureaucracy on the French model. But it is not a convincing political entity. And that is what the promoters of the "single currency" operation always dream of making of it.

Indeed, that is the ambition that Schlesinger, in the conclusion of his article, assigns to the monetary union. The European countries today are encountering difficulties in regard to competition from emerging economies. And, he affirms, it would be quite a lot worse without the European Union. The monetary union will strengthen the position of the continent in international trade talks, as the EMS did earlier within the framework of GATT, and does today in the World Trade Organization.

Admittedly, joint action is much more problematic when it comes to foreign policy and defense. But, concludes Schlesinger, a shared currency "will amalgamate the nations in an indissoluble community." It will thus call into question every dimension of policy that today is the object of sovereign choice for the Member states.

Here, clearly exposed by one of its architects, is the real objective of the euro plan. It seems quite natural. But is this really the case?

The More, the Better?

The European statist doctrines rest on the idea, which appears obvious to many, that since a state is always advantageous, a larger state is even more effective. It allows, everywhere and always, for better defending the interests of the populations that it encompasses and manages.

This is a typical idea of a state technocrat but is a view that is actually very surprising, in that it goes against all the national and international developments of this end of century. This ideology seems to be a holdover from the time of construction of the great European empires, testimony to the historical delay of ideas relative to facts.

However, the example of the USSR during the past century should at least make us think harder. Did the Soviet empire contribute to improving the lot of the average Russian, or Ukrainian, Balt or Chechen?

And if a larger state is always better, how do we explain the disappearance, since the last world war, of all the large empires that had been formed in the previous century? Why did the German Reich disappear, like the British empire, the French empire, and to a certain extent the American empire or quasi-empire?

Along the same lines, if more State is always better, why are the richest countries as well as those who aspire to joining them seeking every means to reduce the internal dimension of the public sector through privatization? Why do they want absolutely to reduce the financial receipts of these states by reducing taxation? Why do they want also to restrict the public resources by limiting the debt? And why do partisans of the euro, in particular in Germany, want rigid budgetary rules and severe penalties for overrunning the specified deficits limits, rules which guarantee in advance that the states will not spend too much?

Why, finally, if more state is always better, do we observe the disintegration of a certain number of federal states, when the federal formula is reputed to be the least constraining, the most democratic, and the most enlightened as regards political organization? Why, everywhere in the world, do the ethnic, religious and regional minorities aspire to secede, in a trend that calls to mind the movements of national minorities in first half of the 19th century?

In a word, it seems that the justification of European political construct by the obvious superiority of a greater state for the wellbeing of the populations is quite fragile.

In addition, this vague idea leads directly to the extreme solution of a single world state that appears completely utopian to any observer with common sense. Would that also be realizable, simply as a matter of will? Or should we admit that there are objective conditions that permit some official constructions but not others?

If one recognizes the Utopia of the maximum state for what it is, an ideology from another era now past, it should then be admitted that there are factors which make practicable or impracticable the construction of such and such specific state, under the prevailing conditions; that not everything is possible; that the size of a state can be too large as well as too small; that there must exist, in a word, an optimal size for a state in a given geographical context, at one precise moment in history.

Is it necessary that economic reason should give way, as Schlesinger invites us to believe, before "reasons of state"? Nothing is less sure, for the reason of state itself is subject to economic constraints and cannot free itself from that. The state is an organization, or a firm, which consumes resources to provide services. As such, it is subject to comparing costs and benefits, that is, to the imperative of economy of means.

Not all the strategies of State development are equally expensive. The economic cost of some makes them prohibitive for the community, therefore unpopular, and finally impossible to put into operation.

The political and organizational strategy of the super State unfortunately is mute on this aspect of the question. It thus neglects to enter into its accounting the greater cost of greater size.

THE COST OF SIZE

The single state realized on the continental scale would be a Very Great State (VGS), just as there are very large libraries or very high speed trains. It constitutes part of those imposing technocratic projects that fascinate politicians. One can conceive indeed that the management and the civil servants of average sized national states would jump at the career-advancement opportunity of a bureaucratic institution infinitely more vast, which would be third in the world in demographic dimension, exceeded only by China and India, and first in national product per capita. With 280 million inhabitants and a GNP of more than 5,700 billion dollars, hardly less than that of the United States, the VGS would be practically the first-ranking world power.

But would the prospect be as great a stimulant for the continent's employees, investors and consumers as it is it for the technocrats and politicians? In other words, what economic effect would be produced by the new geopolitical entity? Would it contribute to raising Europeans' standard of living?

Economic analysis of firms emphasizes the existence of an optimal size, defined by the variation of costs according to the volume of production that is chosen. We can, in the same way, determine an optimal size for the state, considered as an enterprise producing collective services.

That goes against the usual talk we hear concerning the state. Some are "for," others "against," on principle and without nuance. That implies that the former communists and socialists want a maximum state, which absorbs the totality or the major part of the national product. The latter, the liberals, accept only a minimal state, taking as a starting point the limited role of "night watchman" which it held in the 19th century. Actually there is little chance that either one of these two solutions corresponds to the optimal state.

The State as a Firm

The state is a social institution or more precisely an organization. By this we mean a community of individuals gathered for the production of services or, in the language of modern management theory, a "productive team."

The progression of this analysis of "teams" has consisted, for several years, in broadening the theory's sphere of influence, by applying it to every kind of organizations, private and public, profit-oriented and not-for-profit. All indeed offer goods or services thanks to the use of labor and capital in variable proportions, and according to various dimensions.

The state is a not-for-profit enterprise that provides other producers and consumers, in the geographical area that it controls, with complementary services that are essential to their own activities. Security, first of all, without which all production and consumption become random and difficult to sustain. But also material and intellectual infrastructures such as education, and the various public regulations that institute standards of behavior and (by reducing the costs of exchange in social life) support the production of wealth.

In economic terms, this means that the state is an essential factor of national production, complementary for this reason to all the other means of production.

That being the case, the activity of enterprises operating within the institutional framework of the nation-state is partially dependent on the good management of the latter. More especially given that the state levies taxes to finance itself, and thus affects the decisions of all the economic agents and in particular what their labor supply, and their production of goods.

There exists for the state, as for every enterprise, a level of services that minimizes costs. Production is prone to "economies of scale," i.e. it is carried out initially with increasing output (or at decreasing cost) while the costs then gradually will increase when the produced quantities increase. Too little state will not be able to provide the private sector with the public services that are expected. A too large state will impose too high a tax rate for the amount of services that it provides. There is thus a "good" size for a state, that which will maximize the production of private wealth.

This is the conception held, at any rate, by modern theory, which continues to measure the contribution of the state precisely by the induced growth of national product. The new models of growth integrate the state as a factor of production among others and make it possible to define what is its best size, that which carries economic wealth to its maximum level.

On this point, recent research on the comparative growth rates coincides: it appears that the optimal size of the state itself, except investments and welfare systems, is in the neighborhood of 22 or 23% of the national product, according to authors such as Robert J. Barro[1], Robert E. Hall and Charles I. Jones[2], Gerald W. Scully[3], and Georgios Karras[4].

Whereas traditional liberal theory conceives of only the minimal state and traditional socialist theory only of the maximum state, it is understood today that there is an optimal state and that in practice the size of real states are quite close to this standard.

In this approach, the size of the state is measured only by the volume of its expenditure in proportion to the total production of the country.

However, just as a firm can change size either by increasing its volume of sales to given customers, or by selling a given service to a large number of customers, the state can increase its size either by increasing its tax receipts as a percentage of national product within a given geographical area, or by providing the same level of services to an enlarged geographical unit.

The first strategy is intensive growth. The second is extensive growth.

The Optimal Size of Nations

With identical income per capita, the absolute size of the state of a country of five million inhabitants, measured by the amount of resources which it takes from the economy, is necessarily lower than that of the state in a country of one hundred million inhabitants, even if the first takes 80% of the GDP whereas the second extracts from them, by taxation, only 10%.

This depends on two variables: the size of the nation that it manages, on the one hand, and the share of the national product that it controls, on the other hand. The first variable defines the external size of the state, the second its internal size.

The "external" size of the state (the size of the nation) is a strategic variable, that can be the object of a decision, which leads one to speculate about the optimal size of the nation, i.e. that of the social group and the geographical area that the state manages.

And here is the problem that inevitably confronts the federalists' European strategy. To ask whether a state of continental size would be advantageous is equivalent to asking whether Europe constitutes an "optimal state zone."

From this point of view it is almost certain that the European Union does not constitute such an optimal area. Even if the managers of these states, declaring that their domestic markets are saturated and the path to intensive growth is consequently closed, hope to find new outlets through external growth in the markets of neighboring states, it is more likely that the existing national states have a preferable geographical size from the point of view of efficiency. The traditional nations are certainly closer to the conditions of economic effectiveness than the hypothetical continental nation.

What is a "good" size for an organization? The answer lies somewhere between the advantages offered by economies of scale (when certain factors of production are indivisible), and the diseconomies of scale (such as administrative costs that increase with size).

The economies of scale are manifest in the decline in the average cost of production when the volume of production increases. They derive from the existence, in any organization, of fixed and indivisible costs. This may be the case of a production line in an automobile company, which shows a profit only after manufacturing a few hundred vehicles per day. The average cost decreases with the volume of production, because the fixed cost of the mechanical equipment is divided by a growing number of vehicles produced.

When computers were bulky and very expensive, only large companies and governments had access to them, because only they could spread the cost over a sufficiently large volume of production. The greater organizations were, due to this fact, more efficient than the small ones, which could not use data-processing technology. With the personal computer, a craftsman is now as effective in his data-processing management as a great multinational corporation.

But, seen from another side, if the indivisibility of the production infrastructure give a bonus to great size, the latter also inevitably entails increasing costs. They are the costs of bureaucratic control.

A large company employs a large staff. It is based on several levels of hierarchy. It then has to make sure that each one provides indeed the work for which it is paid and does correctly what the firm requires. This control is more difficult in a great human community than in a small one, because the detection of errors and cheating is much more expensive when there are many actors. Losses of production then grow far more quickly than the number of employees within the organization.

The increase in size will thus go hand in hand with a bureaucratic loss of control, with reduced effectiveness of monitoring, which will permit various forms of waste. It is understood, thus, that theft in department stores represents a considerable percentage of sales, whereas it is negligible for an individual tradesman or the craftsman who has only two or three employees under his command.

Consequently, the indivisibility of production's infrastructure must be very strong to justify the costs of great structures of organization, taking into account the quickly growing cost of bureaucratic management.

When the indivisibility of the production infrastructure decreases, for instance when the firm's fixed investments become cheaper relative to the costs of the other factors of production, the economies of size are also reduced. Then it is no longer advantageous to produce on a large scale in order to spread out the fixed costs over a great number of sold units. When there are no more fixed costs, there is no more advantage of size. The smallest firms are quite as efficient as large firms. They offer, moreover, the advantage of avoiding the costs and losses of efficiency linked to the management bureaucracy.

Since the beginning of the Seventies, the tendency is thus toward reducing the size of corporations. But the factors in question also affect all the other organizations, not-for-profit associations and public organizations, and consequently the conglomerates of public organizations and firms that are the state. There is a general phenomenon of atomization of organizations, or "institutional atomization." This consists of reducing the size of the productive team by focussing on its principal business, "re-specialization," which also involves removing layers of the hierarchy, making them "flat."

The plan of the single state is on a collision course with this trend (which relates to states as much as to all the other forms of productive organizations), while institutional atomization reveals the advantage that lies in reducing external size.

INSTITUTIONAL ATOMIZATION

The European project, and the major European error of this end of century, consists of wanting to build a continental federal state in direct opposition to the organizational trend of "downsizing," the universal search for reduced size. The euro-federalist ambition, conceived in a different era, in an economic context of continuous bureaucratic expansion which no longer applies, does not take account of new optimal sizes which pertain to commercial enterprises and to states as well.

European societies are already among the most statist in the world, since the disappearance of Communism. That they should adopt a geopolitical strategy of external growth, by merging several existing states, and choose to reinforce their overblown public hierarchies with an additional administrative layer, defies common sense; unless they intend to compensate for the increase in their external size by diminishing their internal one.

That is precisely how corporate mergers and acquisitions intend to reduce the overheads of the new firms resulting from the deals. But success has not always been achieved. These large maneuvers appear generally to be a losing proposition for the firm that takes the initiative. And the principal virtue of the tender offer is to change the leadership team of the target firm. It is not clear that that would be the case in the construction of a Super State in Europe, since French political leaders and civil servants cannot claim to replace their German or British homologues in Berlin or London.

On the other hand, they can hope that new supranational administrative layers will create additional prospects for employment and responsibility at the national outlets that have become stagnant.

In that case, the merger of European states would not constitute a tender offer with a view toward restructuring aiming to improve overall efficiency. Rather, it would have to do with the creation of a permanent and institutionalized coalition of nation-states, of a state cartel having the objective of escaping the need for that "downsizing" which affects all contemporary organizations.

The Worldwide Restructuring of Corporations and the Search for Value

Everywhere in the world, under the control of customers and shareholders who demand that the value of their securities holdings appreciate, corporations are being restructured to seek the greatest efficiency through systematic reduction of their size.

Mergers and acquisitions lead to a proliferation of the number of small, specialized firms by briskly dismembering the great diversified groups. This is no longer the hour for conglomerates.

From Taylor to the small firm. From this point of view, the Seventies marked a very important turning point. The long trend which had been pushing for the centralization of production, since the end of the 19th century, came to an end. An opposite trend was established.

Since Ford and Schumpeter, it was thought that giant firms, vertically integrated, which participated in a coherent model of development resting on the mass production of standardized products using specific equipment and technological innovations, made it possible to minimize costs by pouring great quantities of standardized products onto vast markets that were expanding continuously.

American firms thus enjoyed a unique advantage because of their internal market of continental size, naturally protected from external competition by distance, the costs of transport, and the technological advance that size itself had fostered.

Organizing labor according to the principles of Taylor (or Ford) was the key to prosperity. It consisted in dividing the tasks, to put them within the capability of unskilled manual labor within very hierarchical firms, bureaucratically managed, where the personnel was closely supervised. This model of industrial development described well the realities of the corporation until the beginning of the Seventies.[5]

That was the time when David Birch, an economist from Massachusetts Institute of Technology, published a study which made a splash the world over. In his analysis of 1979, *The Job Generation Process*[6], he maintained that the majority of new jobs in the United States were created by small businesses. The trend was confirmed by an OECD study[7]. This report concluded that the net creation of jobs had been particularly strong in small companies during the ten to fifteen preceding years.

Taking up again this study in 1987, Birch noted that 88% of the net job creation in the United States between 1981 and 1985 took place in firms of fewer than twenty employees. Practically the entirety of net job creation was related to enterprises with fewer than one hundred employees.

A more recent study by Gary Loveman of Harvard School Business and Werner Sengenberger of ILO[8] confirms the conclusions of the abundant literature that questions the advantages of great size, mass production, and standardization.

Their data show that for the United States, Japan, France, Germany, Great Britain and Italy, the beginning of the Seventies was marked by a clear increase, expressed as a percentage of total employment, of enterprises having respectively less than one hundred and less than five hundred employees, as well in the whole of the economy rather than in the industrial sector. And this phenomenon resulted neither from the development of service activities, nor from the deceleration or acceleration of growth.

Long historical series, extending to 1882 and 1902 respectively for Germany and the United States, show inversely a regular decrease in employment among small firms, a trend that continued until 1970. It was the era of the growth in size of productive organizations.

The spectacular reversal that occurred recently in favor of small and very small firms appears to be confirmed today. The advantage of large companies is a concept of the past.

Flexible specialization is replacing mass production. It is as much the result of small independent firms as that of the decentralization of the larger ones. Radical reorganization breaks up the giant firms into a myriad of small firms that decide their own strategy, even if their capital assets belong to the same parent company. Subcontracting and vertical disintegration are carried out to a previously unknown extent.

The phenomenon has broad scale and important consequences. They affect the style of management and the operating mode of every organization. The process of decision-making and control, which correspond to the traditional hierarchy ("top-down"), is replaced more and more by initiative from below ("bottom up"). Thus we go from "monarchy" to "the republic," a development which we will also find in the fields of politics and administration.

The return to specialization. The mergers and acquisitions of the Eighties and thereafter thus offer a complete contrast with those of the Fifties and Sixties. It is no longer a question of buying up disparate firms to constitute heterogeneous industrial empires. The fashion is no longer the "star system," carrying at the pinnacle star performing managers supposed to have exceptional capacities which enable them to manage air transport companies as well as data-processing firms and film studios. The watchwords of the Nineties are "refocusing" and "chop shop." In other words, cutting up the diversified companies and centering on the principal trade.

In October 1987 a conference organized by the Federal Reserve Bank of Boston, and devoted to the waves of corporate mergers, was held in the small village of Melvin, in New Hampshire. The general acquisition trend since then has evolved into restructuring, the resale of subsidiaries and operational divisions, and the reduction of the number of jobs and in particular of those of the junior staff. This is attributed to the pressure of international competition.

These transactions of great magnitude, financed by debt, often result in "hostile" tender offers, that is, offers refused by the existing managers who fear for their "acquired advantages." The offering party, as a result, has to enhance the stock values and bring considerable profits to the shareholders.

The balance of power within the corporation is deeply upset. The owners now exert increased control over the salaried managers. It is the end, perhaps temporarily, of the "era of managers" described by Burnham as well as Berle and Means in the Thirties, which resulted in an appreciable deterioration of the firms' performance[9]. Then we see capital return to power and less "managerial capitalism," whereby enterprises are managed, according to their personal interests, by management who was concerned rather little with their shareholders.

The new capitalism of the Nineties exerts a much stronger pressure on paid management. It appears that managers react to any takeover threat by abolishing the less profitable divisions themselves, by selling off the less efficient subsidiaries and by devoting more effort to the company's fundamental business[10], an attitude which is due to the intensifying competition and the information and communications revolution.

The change does not seem to be tied to a sudden concern for better management which would affect simultaneously every manager of the enterprise, even the least conscientious or well trained. It results from increased competition on the markets for goods and services that increase the pressure on managers. The least shortcoming on the part of management is translated, much more quickly than in the past, into a disaffection of the consumers who turn toward the products of rival firms.

At the same time, competition on the capital market also intensifies, in particular because of the international breadth of the markets accompanied by the rise to power of the institutional management of savings and investment. Enormous pension funds, which manage the capital accumulated for retirement, put the managers of companies across the whole planet in competition with each other.

But there are also technological reasons for the growing success of small firms. We have cited above the role of the indivisibility of production's infrastructure in defining organizations' economies of size. The revolution of data processing and data communication abolishes or sharply reduces these economies of scale. Batch production is today as powerful as, or more powerful than, mass production. Large markets and large companies no longer dominate the economic landscape.

Considerable progress realized in information storage, processing and transmission have taken us into a society where information is superabundant, which means cheap. Everyone uses it in greater quantities because its cost has fallen vertiginously. Computer memory is increasingly vast and access time is reduced. The Internet, mobile telephones and specialized databases change the conditions of production.

One of the decisive advantages of the large company had to do with its having the means of obtaining very expensive information, whose purchase or internal production represented a massive indivisibility. Now, the drop in cost of information benefits the small firms and is another factor in the abolishment or reduction of the economies of size.

Indeed, the enterprise is, essentially, a center of information production and storage. It makes it possible to accumulate and save information, by centralizing it to use it economically. From this point of view it may be seen as an economic mechanism rivaling that of the market.

The market also makes it possible to produce, use and present information, in particular through the prices and quantities exchanged. But it also calls for flows, far more numerous, diversified and complex than those within the corporations, which is, in sum a machine for saving as much information as possible within the company. The market, by contrast, is an enormous user and producer of information, as Friedrich A. Hayek showed in a famous article[11].

When the cost of information goes down, corporations become

relatively less advantageous, for there is less incentive to save a resource that has become superabundant and then they tend to contract while the markets multiply. There is a movement then toward disintegration of corporations ("downsizing") and the development of "outsourcing," in which the productive relations are taking place more on markets instead of taking place mainly within the large organizational entities, managed according to hierarchical rules, which are corporations.

These fundamental developments have major consequences for social and political equilibrium. Every enterprise and organization is affected by these transformations. However, the hierarchical organization is characterized by a fundamental conflict, an inevitable divergence between the interests of the managers and those of the owners or the principals.

In corporate theory, this divergence is called the "agency problem." The paid manager, not deriving any direct advantage from enhancing the value of the company's equity, may prefer to grow the firm, his "kingdom," which gives him prestige and a social role as well as wages that increase in size, rather than to seek profit as his first priority, which remunerates the shareholder-owner.

The great size of corporations, obtained in particular by diversification, thus corresponds fundamentally to the interest of the managers, not necessarily to that of the shareholders. Under the economic conditions before 1970, the presence of massive economies of scale coincided with the great size of the firm and with profit. But that is not valid any more in the current era. The conflict between management and shareholders has thus become gradually more acute.

Reduced company size allows a greater transparency of management, more especially as it results from a greater abundance of information. Consequently, it leads to better information for shareholders and to closer control over management decisions. It is the increased control by the former that impels the latter to seek profitability as a priority, to focus on core business, and to reduce size, all transactions that benefit the shareholder.

The same applies to productive organizations such as states. Progress in information technologies and international competition have the effect of reducing management's power, fostering the drive to reduce size, strategies which prove favorable to the interests of the customer-owners who are the citizen-voters.

The atomization of states is the precise political equivalent of the atomization of business enterprises.

The Secession Economy

Throughout the ensemble of the industrial States, we see the same tendency toward atomization that is upsetting businesses. The number of smaller states is increasing, compared to the larger ones and, at the same time, some of the great states are breaking apart. The restructuring and respecializing of corporations are mirrored by secessions within the great states, and by privatization which leads them to limit the range of services that they produce to those for which they have an undeniable advantage over private firms, that is the sovereign functions or the general administration of the nation.

If we conceive the ensemble of states which exist in the world as an ensemble of firms producing the same public services for regional or local "customers," we observe the same phenomena as those which affect every corporation and every sector. The average size of companies tends to be reduced, their organization tends to become less hierarchical, "flatter," and the sector's overall degree of concentration decreases. The big conglomerates are disappearing, splitting up.

For the world industry of state-conglomerates, the beginning of the century, by contrast, was characterized by increasing concentration obtained through external growth. This led, at the conclusion of the Second World War, to the "duopoly" of super-powers, the United States and the Soviet Union—after the elimination of the two other great powers, the Axis nations, Germany and Japan.

As for the internal size of the political entities, the period also lent itself to sustained high growth through diversification of activities, reaching its climax with the absorption of all of the society's other activities of production (in the case of Communism), or in total statism (Fascism). In economic terms, it was a movement of conglomerate concentration of the activity of the sector.

But the period of returning to international open trade that followed the end of the conflict was marked by an inverse trend, with a deconcentration of the world's industry of nation-states, in spite of the continuation of a cold war between the two super-powers and their allies and their empires.

An industry becomes less concentrated when the number of firms increases, and at the same time, when there is a relative reduction of the largest producers' share in the sector, either because of the growth of the number of smaller firms, or because they increased in size through internal growth, while the size of the largest was reduced.

For nation-states, which together constitute the population of this industry, the reduction in the degree of concentration will result in the decline of the relative weight of largest.

The Increase in the Number of States. The number of independent nation-states existing in the world went from 74 in 1946 to 192 in 1995. In economic terms, that corresponds to an "atomization" of the population of the enterprises considered. When the number of producers in a given industry increases significantly, one usually says that the supply becomes "atomistic," that is, very competitive.

In fact, many of the new states are "enterprises" of very small size. In 1995, 87 of the 192 states existing in the world had fewer than 5 million inhabitants. And among those, 58 had fewer than 2.5 million inhabitants, and 35 fewer than 500,000 nationals.

A number of new countries which were created out of the remnants of the old Soviet Union are in this position. Latvia, for example, has only 1.7 million inhabitants, Turkmenistan 4 million, Moldova 4.5 million, and Kyrghyzstan 4.8 million. More than half of the countries in the world (98 nations) have a demographic size smaller than the American state of Massachusetts, which had 6 million inhabitants in 1990, which is also the "median" size of the state enterprise.

This atomization of the "industry of states" arises to some extent from the disintegration of empires, in particular during the decolonization of Africa but also more recently with the implosion of the USSR. Most spectacular, without question, was the pure and simple disappearance of the Soviet Union. But, since this left the United States as the only super power in the running, this masked her loss of relative power.

We are, indeed, witnessing the decline of the importance of the United States in the world, as an economic power and as an empire.

From the economic point of view it is clear that other nations' accelerated development, in Europe and Japan in the post-war period, then in the newly industrialized countries more recently, and currently even in China, diminished the proportion of the United States in world economic production. It is the phenomenon of the latecomers catching up to the economically most advanced countries.

Where the American national product represented, in 1948, a little more than 30% of the world GNP, it no longer represented any more than 24% in 1992; and the trend continues[12].

Moreover, not all the countries with a lower standard of living have succeeded yet to launch themselves into sustained growth. This depends on a certain number of initial political and economic conditions: manpower training, opening the economy to international trade, a "reasonable" policy of debt and taxation by the state. Catching up seems possible and manifest only when you start from a level of GDP per capita above a minimum, as has been noted by Hall and Jones, Barro, and other theoreticians of economic growth. But when it is seriously started, it becomes inevitable, whenever the cost of imitation is less than the cost of innovation. The United States undoubtedly remains the most creative country in the world, and one of the richest, but their task is much more difficult than that of the followers who, in increasing numbers, imitate them.

In international politics, they do not escape the disappearance of their empire any more than the other great powers did before them. The phenomenon is less obvious than in the case of France or the Soviet Union, because membership in the American sphere took more various and less obvious forms. But it is no less real, as Leonard Dudley[13], in particular, shows. And if America's international influence remains considerable, even though difficult to measure, it is, however, clear that it was put in check by smaller countries like Vietnam and Iran.

If one takes the club of great powers of 1945 it appears, fifty years later, that their economic and military weight over the rest of the world tends to decrease and that this development will continue with the diffusion of technical progress and economic growth to the whole planet.

The global industry of states thus undergoes a double movement toward deconcentration, on the one hand because of the latecomers' catching up economically to the dominant states, and on the other hand because of the disintegration of great states which split up to be replaced by several state firms of smaller size.

One thus observes an unquestionable trend toward fragmentation of states that are both significant in size and characterized by the grouping together of dissimilar economic components. That is also valid for small states whose population and culture are particularly heterogeneous.

The creation of small states, just like the disintegration of empires, can be explained by the set of economic factors such as the development of world markets with trade liberalization, but also by the increasing social cost of national taxation in a world of mobile goods and people. Finally, the new abundance of information reduces the comparative advantage of the great states, just as it reduces that of large corporations.

With the opening and the liberalization of world trade, desired by the United States and the United Nations after 1945, it became possible for the ethnic minorities within heterogeneous states to take their independence without suffering a decline in standard of living. Instead of relying exclusively on the large accessible markets within the great nation or the empire to which they belonged, they can have access freely and directly to the great world market or to the many markets of the nations which take part in the system of free trade.

The enterprises of the small nations, or the micro-nations, can thus be as efficient as those of the large countries because the world markets enable them to achieve the minimal size which makes it possible to be efficient, while at the same time their national market is of very small size.

Regional and cultural minorities can thus "afford the luxury" of secession because the political borders no longer coincide with market areas. The globalization of trade thus tends to cause a trend of political disintegration and secession.

Moreover, the opening of the economies and the mobility of the factors of production which accompanies it, with regard to labor as well as to capital, reduces the states' power to tax. It is difficult to bear down on specialists who can easily find work in other countries, or on capital, which can leave the country instantaneously to emigrate toward more lenient tax environments.

The states' ability to extract taxes thus tends to decrease even when the tax basis is unchanged, because of increasing legal loopholes resulting from increased international mobility—which obliges states to reduce their spending, or at least not to increase it. It is natural under these conditions to question expenditures carried out in the nation's least central territories. That initially affects an empire's protectorates, the overseas territories, and the most distant frontier areas.

Spending cuts on the part of the nation, including for maintenance of law and order and the armed forces, fosters the rise of independence movements. And that propels the "downsizing" of nation-states.

One can indeed conceive the demographic or geographical size of a state as resulting from a trade-off between the economies which result from the fact that one can spread out the expenditure corresponding to the public benefits over a wider population of taxpayers, on the one hand, and the increasing costs of production of these same collective benefits to an increasingly large, and thus probably increasingly heterogeneous, population, on the other.

National defense provides a good example where economy of scale favors a state of great size. An investment as massive as the acquisition of nuclear weapons can be borne only by a very large number of taxpayers, so that the per capita burden is moderate. Thus, a military investment of 200 billion dollars will cost 1 million per capita for the taxpayer in a country of 200,000 inhabitants, but only 10,000 dollars per capita in a country of 20 million inhabitants, and the more modest sum of 1,000 dollars per taxpayer in a country of 200 million inhabitants.

This is why Albania cannot procure the same modern nuclear armaments as France, or *a fortiori* as the United States. The same applies to such collective investments as a legal, educational, or monetary system.

The greater the number of investors and consumers who use a currency, the better it is. This is why a currency is almost always issued by a state. The state makes the use of its currency compulsory to all its citizens, which provides a captive market and *a priori* gives this currency an advantage over other instruments which, dependent on an individual's free choice, will be less widespread and will not benefit from this initial advantage.

But from another perspective, for many collective goods, serving more numerous populations also means serving more heterogeneous populations. And that increases the cost of producing the collective services. Thus, a common legal system is far more expensive when it is provided for populations which do not speak the same language, compared to when it is implemented for only one speech community. From this point of view the cost of an empire or a multinational or multi-ethnic federation is higher than that of a single nation. One may consider, for example, the cost of the bureaucratic management of the European Community, if only because of the need to translate the debates and official documents into several languages.

One of the reasons why the performance of the small nations has been so satisfactory in recent times lies in the fact that the savings from spreading the costs of the collective goods over vast populations has probably decreased with the progress of technology. Many small countries have nuclear weapons today, if only under license, even "second hand," whereas in 1944 only the immense American power could handle the enormous expenditure required to design and build them. In the same way the computer, which was within reach only for the world's largest organizations in the Fifties, today is available at low prices to any private individual. The "indivisibility" of investment tends to disappear, making small organizations more competitive compared to the largest, as we have already seen.

National defense is a case in point. If indivisibilities were strong there, the largest countries would spend less, expressed as a percentage of their national product, than small countries. However, in point of fact there is no relationship between county size and the ratio of military expenditure to GDP.

Of course, in certain regards it is inefficient for a state wishing to be sovereign to be too small: Monaco cannot declare war with France. But on the other hand, recent military history, in particular that of the French decolonization but also that of Vietnam and Afghanistan, indeed showed that size is no longer a decisive factor of military power. That has facilitated wars of independence, and secessions. The economies of size are no longer what they once were, when it comes to producing collective benefits.

That brings us to contemporary musings on the future of nation-states. A recent article published in the *International Herald Tribune*[14], reporting on a conference on this topic organized in Salzburg, was entitled in a significant and provocative way: "Does the nation-state still have a future?" The question on the table was whether this specific form of social organization, created five centuries ago, was today on the verge of relinquishing the throne and giving way to regional entities within a global society characterized by tribal and ethnic competition. The conference participants did not go that far. They thought it possible that in the immediate future, in the 21st century, there could be four hundred independent nations in the world.

All that results from the combination of globalization and the information and communications revolution. Today, multinational corporations assemble goods whose components come from factories based everywhere in the world. The central processing unit of the computer on which I write these lines was manufactured in Scotland. The screen comes from Singapore and the internal microprocessors from the United States. The printer is imported from Taiwan.

In the services too, legal, accounting, advertising, computer consulting, it seems that the world has abolished the national borders. In Moscow, large American and European consulting firms are helping the Russian government as well as the local subsidiaries of German, American and Japanese firms.

The financial markets are globalized. Where the nation-states formerly tried to fix the exchange rates, individual operators now determine movements of capital at the incredible rate of 1.3 trillion (1300 billion) dollars per day.

These factors are leading the largest, and therefore the most heterogeneous, nation-states to be called into question. The most spectacular case was that of the USSR. The reason was simple, in the end. In permanent and intense competition with the United States, the USSR had to invest massively in military industries and defense. However, its centralized economy was less efficient in the long term than that of the United States, which was decentralized and private. The USSR generated a smaller production of wealth and consequently little tax resources for the central state. That forced its leaders to sacrifice other provisions of public services. In addition, the heterogeneity of the populations was much stronger in the Soviet empire than in the fifty states of America. That entails greater costs for management and control. Finally, the USSR disintegrated because it went bankrupt: it was no longer able to pay its army nor to maintain order in the satellite countries, or even in its own interior territories peopled with ethnic minorities. Each constituent nation then seized the idea of creating its own state while opening up to international markets.

Other countries followed the same path. Yugoslavia was propelled into civil war due to the complex, even inextricable geographical overlapping of populations of different ethnic groups. But also Czechoslovakia, which solved the problem peacefully because of the very clear geographical and economic separation of the Czechs and the Slovaks.

Centrifugal tendencies can also be observed in Ireland, in Spain, and Italy. In Canada, traditionally strained by cultural and linguistic tensions, the 1997 elections were marked by extreme ethnic and regional polarization. Three principal parties, the party of the new democracy on the left, liberals in the center, and the conservative progressive party on the right, ended up representing specific areas almost exclusively. Thus the liberals obtained two thirds of their seats in only one province, Ontario, sweeping up 101 seats out of the 105 available to the province. In Quebec, the Quebec Bloc took the majority of seats. In the western provinces the reform party, which is especially anti-Quebec, secured 70% of the seats, while winning only one in the other areas of the country. In sum, Canada is on the point of fracturing into several separate pieces.

Should America be Dismembered? A similar debate on the virtues of secession is conducted even in the United States, whose federal unity seemed until now safe from any criticism.

In a remarkable article published in November-December 1994 in the magazine *Challenge,* Thomas Naylor, who was professor of economy and management at Duke University, poses the shocking and taboo question in a country which has known a War of Secession: it is time to dismember America?

The essence of his argumentation is that, just as the Soviet Union had become "unmanageable," for it was impossible to satisfy 285 million individuals from a central office installed in Moscow, in the same way China, Japan, India, Brazil and the United States are no longer manageable in their current forms. Just as Mikhail Gorbachev noted the impossibility of leading the USSR from its capital, according to the author, the White House and Congress also acknowledge that it is futile to try to impose solutions concocted by federal bureaucrats from the top, from Washington, on the problems of poverty, homelessness, racism, drugs, crime and failing schools.

It is, furthermore, the same kind of report which is made in Europe in connection with the Brussels regulations on hunting and fishing in Languedoc, or the standards for cheese manufacturing. One may also refer to the difficulty, that is, the high cost, of the management of immense bureaucracies like the Red Army, which was the largest in the world in terms of the number of people employed, or the world's second bureaucracy by rank of size, which is the French National Ministry of Education.

Solutions can be found and put in action only locally, in order to take into account the specific requests of the consumers. The United States in particular is too vast and too varied for the problems of Los Angeles and Chicago to bare scarcely any relationship to those of

Texas, Vermont, Oregon or the Mississippi delta. The inhabitants of Richmond, Virginia are completely indifferent to the problems of Harlem, and vice versa. Attempts to create loyalties and bonds, financed by taxes, are thus both ineffective and expensive, and moreover are poorly accepted politically because of the voters' indifference for the residents of other cities located in too distant states.

There is no real meaning to membership in the same community shared between the inhabitants of fifty disjointed states. That contrasts distinctly with the situation in Switzerland, Austria, Finland, Norway and Sweden, even in Singapore. Those are communities of limited size whose members can still experience a feeling of common membership.

One can certainly object that the heterogeneity of the United States is not new. What changed, rather, are the reasons that drove the states to unite, as well as the relative advantages of union compared to independence. The disappearance of the Soviet threat lessened the already discounted utility of the central state and fully revealed the disadvantages of heterogeneity. The federal state's raison d'être seems weak or non-existent today, according to Naylor, in spite of the efforts expended, during the Gulf War in particular, to make Iraq the successor of the USSR in the role of the external enemy threatening the United States' safety.

What is necessary today, according to Naylor, is a radical solution: secession. States such as Alaska, Hawaii, Oregon and Vermont should be allowed to leave the Union, each state having to calculate the cost-benefits of its participation in the financing of the federal state. Vermont, for example, contributed as much as 80 million dollars toward financing the rescue of the savings and loans, which cost on the whole 500 billion. Was it worth it? Idaho and the state of Washington are currently financing the Los Angeles water supply, and complaining bitterly. Is this really necessary?

Secession would not relate only to the great states—like California, which holds nearly 31 million inhabitants, or the state of New York with 18.1 million, or Texas which encompasses 17.7 million, or Florida with its 13.5 million residents. These states themselves could find an advantage in internal fragmentation. California could separate into three independent states. And cities like New York, Washington DC, Los Angeles, Houston and Miami might find it advantageous to disintegrate into several smaller local communities.

To replace the current federation by a looser confederation between more or less independent states could well be an advantageous solution for all.

It is against this backdrop that we must consider the European federalist enterprise inherited from the reconstruction period of the Fifties, marked by the Cold War and the Soviet threat. Is it really necessary to create a continental Super State to integrate 350 million Europeans who already have nation-states of imposing size, whereas everywhere else the tendency to disintegration continues?

Would such a superstructure be likely to improve the lot of the various populations concerned? That would require that it, and only it, be able to offer new services that the existing nation-states could not provide, or that they would provide poorly.

That is the contention of the Super State advocates—that only this would guarantee peace among the states in Europe and defend our continent in the international commercial war.

ILLUSORY ADVANTAGES

Of course, we see in the world as it is states that survive with greatly different sizes, from Switzerland to the United States, not to mention Singapore and China. Above and below the median value of 6 million inhabitants in 1990, states of very diverse demographic size are spread into equal quantities, which is explained by the diverse degree of homogeneity of the population (ethnic, cultural, linguistic, and religious), by the geographic conditions and the transportation costs, by the intensity of the economic ties with near or distant nations, by the greater or lesser degree of openness of the economy and by each country's political regime.

In Europe itself, without counting Luxembourg, the sizes are ranked between Ireland and Denmark, which respectively hold 3.6 and 5.2 million inhabitants, and France, Great Britain, Italy and Germany which exceed 50 million.

The geography of each state must correspond to a principle of optimization as we saw above, even if this optimization was not arrived at through any deliberated calculation. The "principle of the survivor," that the Nobel Prize laureate in economics George Stigler applied to firms and that the biologists know well, suggests indeed that the species or the individuals who survive in an environment characterized by competition for scarce resources are those that are better adapted to their milieu, be that only of a simple ecological "niche." The Soviet Union disappeared due to generalized inefficiency, but the small states that thrive must probably have certain competitive advantages.

But besides pure size, other factors weigh more directly against the construction of a Very Great continental state. Compared to the United States, for example, it is banal to note that Europe is more heterogeneous linguistically and culturally, which implies a high cost for producing state services, while at the same time it is already overly state-controlled and at a considerable cost. The transfers carried out through the regional policy of the European Union are at least as indifferent to the resident of Hamburg, when the recipients are Neapolitan, as to the inhabitant of Richmond when they are given to residents of Harlem. Conversely, the centralized regulations of Brussels cause dissatisfaction and protests in Normandy as well as in Calabria.

But especially, the political and economic advantages invoked in favor of a Super State do not correspond to the conclusions that one may draw from an analysis of the global industry of states. This is as true with regard to the risk of war between European natinos as for the potential advantages the continent would derive from its unity, in the global commercial war between continental areas that some see on our doorstep—an argument that Helmut Schlesinger in particular calls upon in the article previously cited.

Two political arguments in favor of the Super State constitute, in fact, two illusory advantages: that it would guarantee peace in Europe, on the one hand, and that it would make it possible to wage commercial war externally, on the other.

Peace through Union?

Atomization of states reduces the probability of conflict between them—which appreciably weakens the argument in favor of a great European State. Nobody accepts any more the prospect of new Franco-German wars, but the possibility of such a conflict is very often invoked to justify a federal union built around the single currency.

The argument is superficial. First, because civil wars do exist, and are even particularly frequent within heterogeneous federal states. If, by chance, for a reason difficult to imagine today, major conflicts of interests arose between France and Germany, what in the future would prevent them from expressing themselves within a European federation in the same way as the conflict between Russia and the Chechens or Serbia, Croatia and Bosnia within the framework of the former Yugoslavia?

In addition, modern analysts of international politics, like Edward Mansfield[15], show that the probability of interstate wars increases with the concentration of states. When, on the contrary, their global industry disintegrates, and is decentralized, as is the case now at the end of the century, the probability of wars between them is lowered.

Indeed, the motivation to extend the external size of states tends to disappear when the latter seek as a priority to reduce their size and to contract their geographical surface. That is not the hour for the constitution of empires and the conflicts of interests that they cause between expanding great nations. Rather, the question today, for a state, is of an internal nature: must it accept that such and such of its regions secedes? But states in the course of contraction or dismantling are not on a collision course with other states engaged in a similar process.

The question was obscured by the Russian-American Cold War, which led to the division of many countries bordering on the respective areas of influence, into one favorable to the United States and another favorable to the USSR. There was thus a positive correlation between the (cold) war and the decomposition of the states, the latter being a result of the former.

But today an underlying and fundamental tendency to split up has appeared, which no longer owes anything to a cold war that is now finished. In its place, "autonomous" or "endogenous" wars of secession appear and multiply, due to the new economic conditions under which the state-enterprises are managed.

The conclusion is highly significant for the attempt at a European merger. Contrary to the often-expressed fear, the risk of interstate war will decrease in Europe, as elsewhere in the world, as the countries of the continent disintegrate—whereas it could well reappear during a phase of concentration of national states into heterogeneous entities or empires, which would obtain only a dubious loyalty from the populations concerned.

The conflicts disappeared once Yugoslavia broke up into Slovenia, Croatia, Bosnia and Serbia. They would disappear tomorrow if Ulster separated from Great Britain and the Basque Country seceded from Spain.

By contrast, what threatens to create serious confrontations at the national level is indeed the integration of the European nations within a single state managing a single currency. We see the first steps of this today in the clashes over economic and monetary management, as Bernard Connolly analyzed so well in his book, *The Dirty War of the European Currency*[16].

A single Europe would cause future internal conflicts, while not contributing to the reduction of the risks of war between existing nations, risks that are already naturally reduced because of the global devolution of the industry of States.

The virtues of the European Super State for maintaining peace thus appear singularly exaggerated.

Winning the International Commercial War?

It is quite as doubtful, or is at the very least an exaggeration, to believe, as many do, that Europe, which is not an optimal monetary area or an optimal administrative zone, could be an optimal commercial zone.

We know that in the Eighties, among other fundamental transformations of the world economy, regional free trade zones were developed, as well as other preferential arrangements concerning international trade. Alongside the European Economic Community, the oldest, the Association of South-East Asian Nations (ASEAN), and the free trade agreement between the United States and Canada, were established. In 1992 the latter was extended to the whole North American continent, by including Mexico (NAFTA). The world is thus compartmentalized into three continental commercial areas centered around the United States, Europe and Japan. And trade in the Eighties developed more quickly inside these areas than between these areas or with other countries.

Compared to the general principle that holds that free trade increases the wellbeing of all the nations that adhere to it, these commercial zones appear relatively harmful. But at the same time they can be presented as an intermediate phase on the way to global free trade.

The commercial policy of these regional blocks decisively affects how we judge them. Is Europe a protectionist "fortress," as the Americans claim, or on the contrary an open market (or a "sieve") as European politicians and CEOs maintain? Is the United States itself a sincere champion of global free trade or on the contrary unscrupulously protectionist, using their "Super 301" legislation to set up, practically at their own discretion, any trade barriers they wish for such and such industry, under the pretext of unfair competition from a foreign country?

And if the economists are, in their overwhelming majority, in favor of free trade, they often recognize that social regulations that are so different between trade partners (such as, for example child labor laws or the lack of any health care protection) that countries can pose problems of unfair competition or "social dumping," justifying in part a more selective commercial policy.

From this point of view of confrontation between continental blocks and major differences in the rules of the game, "commercial war," i.e. protectionism makes sense. It is important then to be able to counter-attack, to negotiate, instead of unilaterally lowering duties and non-tariff trade barriers.

A single European authority to negotiate the external commercial policy is then useful. It will be all the more effective if the economy to which it is applied is a significant player in world trade and can therefore influence international prices. In this case, protectionist calculations can prove to pay off by reducing, via higher tariffs, the demand for imports, which causes a decline of world prices that ultimately will benefit the big protectionist country. Such an aggressive commercial policy may be advantageous for a large commercial area, but the profit obtained is paid via costs inflicted on the exporting country.

There is, however, a second argument in favor of the regional commercial zone, if one takes into account the transport costs of international trade.

Low or nonexistent transport costs would lead to the superiority of global free trade. On the contrary, very high costs encourage more trade with immediate geographical neighbors. In this case, a regional free trade area can constitute the most advantageous solution for all because global free trade, which entails high transport charges, is actually not optimal.

In reality, regional commercial areas can address both these two types of objectives, one of commercial war, the other of realizing a practicable form of free trade.

One can figure what is the current policy of Europe by estimating the share of internal exchanges within the area that is warranted by transport costs. If the intensity of the actual trade exceeds this "natural" level, then the area is conducting an offensive policy of protectionist warfare.

According to recent calculations, that is the case of the European Union[17]. Far from being an open market, Europe is already an aggressive player in the international commercial war. The argument of the market clout, which a Great European State would provide, then tends to lose impact, since this policy is already implemented by the European Union, even without a unified continental state. Thus there is no need whatsoever to build a European Super State to achieve the goal of international trade negotiation.

In addition, taking into account the various costs that would result from a single state, any profit from it probably would be negligible. This is especially true if one takes into account the unforeseeable costs of commercial war, which can lead the partner countries to react by protectionist measures, thus ratcheting up retaliatory forms of protection.

In a world undergoing the process of globalization, a regional commercial area can be an instrument of defense against international competition and free trade. There can thus be interest "to think commercial war" in an imperfect world where commercial zones exist which aggressively negotiate the conditions of exchange while using their economic weight to obtain the lion's share in the division of the gains of the exchange.

But the example of small countries that succeed in international trade shows that it is not necessarily a dominant strategy.

Finally, the advantages of the Super State for maintaining peace in Europe or in waging commercial war appear illusory. It offers no exclusive advantage that the national states cannot obtain by themselves. On the other hand, the disadvantages that it presents because of the additional burden of the hierarchical structures inherent in its size are, in themselves, quite real. And far from replacing then national bureaucracies, the Super State is more likely to add administrative layers to the already heavy and overly expensive national pyramids.

A STIFLING SUPERSTRUCTURE

Will the construction of a Very Great European State mark, in a surprising paradox, the beginning of the decline of the state on the continent? That is what the monetary federalists have the nerve to suggest. In cooperation with the regional authorities of each member state, the administrative machinery of Brussels would replace the national bureaucracies, whose role would gradually melt away.

Thus the VGS would substitute for the national states in accordance with the general principle of "subsidiarity." In euro-speak, this term means that the European State would do nothing that cannot be achieved by the national states. That corresponds to a concern for fundamental coherence between various levels of responsibility within the same ensemble of administrative hierarchies but does not necessarily constitute a practical guarantee.

The euro-statists tell us that the constitution of a continental Super State will make it possible to reduce the weight of the national state in the society, its internal size, compared to that which exists today on the continent. According to them the federal state necessarily will be light, since the populations' assent to its development is weak. At the same time it will initiate a direct dialogue with the regions inside the European nations, to some extent short-circuiting the national states. The latter gradually losing their functions, upwards in favor of the continental Super State, for example for defense and diplomacy, and downwards, in favor of their regional authorities as regards the daily tasks of general administration, will be brought to collapse. The natural attrition of the national state, a Marxist prophecy whose failure in this century is well known, may finally be realized.

At the same time, the development of the large market being accompanied by a reduction of the national administrative structures, the construction of a Super State in Europe would appear an eminently liberal pro-market enterprise!

We have seen, however, that there is actually no field reserved to the European State in which it would achieve tasks that the current states are not able to carry out very well. Under these conditions the European bureaucracy and the national bureaucracies will tend to do the same things twice, as we see already with the repeated interference of the former in the jurisdiction of the latter, allegedly in the interest of standardizing legislation and unifying the market. The respective jurisdictions overlap and will continue to do so, involving a redundancy of bureaucratic hierarchies.

The question is fundamental, given the urgent need to restructure all the welfare states of the continent. However, a bureaucratic super-hierarchy would be at cross-purposes with the needs, given that the most massive hierarchies are also the heaviest to manage and, due to natural inertia, the most conservative.

Why then does Europe, which has such difficulty in reducing the internal size of its states continue seeking to resolve its problems by increasing its external size? Why build a continental Super State which, in turn, will increase the overall internal size of its bureaucracy?

The phenomenon is explained, as we have already seen, by the persistence of old ideas and national ambitions, in France as in Germany. But it also arises from the will to create a new field of expansion for the bureaucracy at a moment when the globalization of the economy erodes the tax resources of the national states and imposes upon them the prospect of an inevitable contraction of their activities. That directly results in a deterioration of the career-advancement opportunities of the civil servants and politicians within nations. This is why it is, first and foremost, a question of increasing the size of the heavy bureaucratic apparatus on a given territory and population.

But as a consequence, we will have to finance the additional activities of the civil servants of Brussels and Strasbourg by increased taxes. Modest today, they will be heavier tomorrow if the continental bureaucracy must be clothed and fed. Under these conditions, can one expect the tax pressure exerted in the name of the national state to diminish? That seems doubtful at best. Public bureaucracies seldom die and almost never shrink.

The Inevitable Proliferation of Hierarchies

The example of regional reform in France is a good illustration. It was launched as an exercise in decentralization, which had become essential, given that the state was judged to have become suffocating and sclerotic. The argument in this case, too, consisted of a promise to compensate with a reduction of the national bureaucratic apparatus. A more efficient regional public administration, closer to the citizens, would be substituted for the central state in the achievement of a great number of tasks, and the State hierarchy could consequently reduce its size and the tax burden.

The outcome is well known. Now we have both the Central State and the Regional authorities. They added a hierarchical level to the existing political apparatus. And regional tax regimes, rapidly increasing, bear a good share of the responsibility for the growing fiscal burden experienced in recent years.

It may be that the citizens are better served by this increase of administrative and political supply. But it is contrary to the truth and to the most elementary common sense to claim that multiplication of hierarchical levels can bring about an overall reduction of administrative organization.

Furthermore, this experience corresponds to the famous politico-humorous "law" stated by C. Northcote Parkinson: bureaucracies imperturbably continue their expansion even when they have lost their point and their reason for being, such as, for example the administration of the colonies in Great Britain after the war, while the British Empire was fading away[18]. Administrative organizations are immortal.

The reason for this apparent nonsense lies in the conflict, mentioned above and known as "the agency problem," which in any organization pits the managers (the agents) against the owners (or principals). The interest of the manager is related to the size and growth of his organization. The managerial objective is thus always and primarily growth, the construction of an empire and the desire for power ("hubris").

In the Interest of the Civil Servants. No easy promotion is possible for managers, nor for average bureaucrats, apart from an extension of their field of activity. A stagnant hierarchy is a hierarchy where promotion, slow and difficult, is reserved to a small number. An expanding hierarchy, on the other hand, represents an open field of opportunity. The number of the levels of monitoring and supervision increases quickly to accommodate a larger staff. Internal promotion is accelerated. Career-advancement opportunities are good, and wages go up.

That is as true for the public bureaucracies as for the private capitalist enterprises. But for the latter, the interest of the shareholders often thwarts the managers' growth targets. If growth no longer results in profits or, worse still, generates losses, the shareholders will sell their shares, the stock prices will drop, and the firm will become vulnerable to a takeover. The management will have to take stock and modify its policy of growth, and devote itself more to the quest for profit. Or else the firm will end by being bought and the manager and his team replaced by other managers, more concerned with enhancing value and less inclined toward growth in its own right.

In the case of the political enterprise that is the State, the owners—the voter-taxpayers—have less control because of the great diversity of the productions of services of this conglomerate enterprise, the absence of an overall indicator of good management such as profit, and because of the high number of "shareholders." When the electorate amounts to a million people, the influence of the individual vote becomes unimportant. Each voter has practically no incentive to inform himself in detail of the quality of governmental management. Ignorance is rational, control is reduced.

This weakness of external control in political enterprises, combined with the great size of the organization, enables the tendency in favor of growth for its own sake to go on long after the economic conditions of management make the large size of the State inefficient. Thus there is every reason to fear that a continental Super State will increase the total weight of the public hierarchies in Europe. European managerialism will be strengthened by it.

"Societal Managerialism." Anyone can see the difference in operation that separates the societies of continental Europe from Great Britain and the United States. This banal report has given rise to the thesis of "two capitalisms" which differentiate themselves in particular by their mode of financing and the extent of the public sector.

An identical model would describe both the German society and the French society. Characterized by the importance of bank financing and the power of the managers and the State, they aim to avoid the "excesses" of the United States' and Great Britain's market capitalism. Public and private managers being opposed to the domination of the market, they would both necessarily defend the interests of the employees linked to social democratic policies.

There are, however, good reasons to think that reality is the opposite. Managers' discretionary power impoverishes the society and slows down economic progress. In fact, the markets and open competition favor wealth creation. And the degree of a society's overall hierarchical concentration is the decisive variable indicating whether the power of the managers in general is under control.

This reflects the importance of hierarchical systems in the social organization, relative to the alternative mechanism of production, the market. As Oliver Williamson[19] emphasized, following the Nobel laureate in Economics, Ronald Coase[20], production can indeed be conducted in a more centralized way, the exchanges and assemblies of components taking place within a large organization, or in a more decentralized way when they rely more on individual producers and small firms interacting on markets which are external to them.

In a society dominated by hierarchies where very large organizations, public and private, are responsible for the bulk of production, the managers are fewer and they hold a considerable social power. Less restricted by the markets, both because the monopolistic power of their organizations increases with size and because their sheer size shelters them from control by the many and scattered shareholders and principals, they can pursue their own interests at their own discretion.

The concentration of hierarchies in the society and the resulting attenuation of competition between fewer managers define the greater or lesser degree of the nation's managerialism.

The "Societal Managerialism" index is crucial because the power of the managers induces a general attitude with regard to reforms and social developments. It also explains the cultural attitudes and the forms that the political development takes.

The opposition of the systems is then between countries with a "single hierarchy" and the "Anglo-Saxon" countries, this division corresponding in practice both to the different degrees of hierarchization and to the systems of financing. In the model of market capitalism, with a low level of hierarchization, the state hardly intervenes in management and control of the companies, which are themselves independent of each other and only report directly to the financial market.

On the contrary, societies that tend toward the centralization of a single hierarchy, public or private, but generally both public and private, give their management a great independence with regard to the markets. Fewer and more autonomous, they are devoted to the practice of inside control within a closed club. This is the social system of managerialism, described in particular by Milovan Djilas in *The New Class* and denounced by John Kenneth Galbraith as the triumph of "technostructure." The first author, however, had in mind only the communist systems while the second felt that it had to do with a shortcoming specific to the American big-business capitalism. In fact it is about a general tendency, more or less visible according to the specific society under consideration.

A system that is strongly managerial gives considerable power to a restricted elite, because the hierarchies, being vast, are very few. Thus there are few true directors. Although these hierarchies can be as well private as public, it is clear that a society where the state is big will have a more markedly managerial character because the State hierarchy is unique. Thus the number of executives will be fewer there than in a society of private firms independent of each other and controlled by the anonymous financial market.

A society where there is but one owner, one hierarchy of organizations, and where competition between potential managers is carried out only within one club, while their turnover depends on only one person, is an extreme example of a managerial society. One will recognize the model of the Soviet Union, with the State ownership of all the firms and the management nomination only by the government, only within the club of the Communist Party members.

By contrast, a society where the renewal of the elites is frequent because competition for access to management positions is very open and diversified will be less managerial than a society where there is only one path to advancement, through a monopoly, and based on a competition that takes place primarily at the beginning of one's career, at school. The mechanism of the takeover bid thus plays an essential part in ensuring the maintenance of strong competition between managers, but this part can also be played by the bank managers— provided that they, themselves, are subject to control and to strong competition!

It follows that the judgement on the overall character of a society, whether more or less managerial, must take into account several elements: the average size of the hierarchies in the society, the concentration of ownership of companies, and the level of competition between, respectively, managers and owners of enterprises.

European societies are very managerial, both because the State apparatuses are larger and because the financial markets have less control over private companies. Thus the public and private hierarchies, on the whole, hold an important place in society relative to the markets.

This model contains alternative forms, that of statist capitalism and that of corporatist capitalism. Japan and France are examples of the first, Germany of the second, and Italy participates in both, with a strong component of family capitalism.

Thus France and Germany, rather differently organized in terms of the respective roles of public and private banking, the organization of the state, and the system of recruiting managers, end up with similar degrees of managerialism. In both countries the number of companies whose shares are quoted on the stock exchange is small. It frequently happens that only one shareholder (a single family or a single industrial firm) holds more than 25% of their capital, and these controlling shareholders exchange participations in reciprocal shareholding. France and Germany are thus characterized by a system of control in the hands of "insiders," that is, a club[21]. These two societies are opposed to the United States and to Great Britain where managers are submitted to far more intense competition, where they are much more mobile and where the owners' interests are defended better.

The respective roles of the banks and the financial markets play only in a secondary way. Recent studies show that the importance of the financial markets in the national economies depends on the legal system of protection of the interests of the owners. Where these interests are defended better, the financial markets are developed. Greater or lesser development of the financial markets may then be explained by the characteristics of the countries' legal culture[22].

The managerial model, which prevails in continental Europe, has been an obstacle to necessary adaptation within each state. Today called into question by the opening of markets and the globalization of communication, it would be reinforced by a continental federal state imposed on the top of the national States. It would then block the fledgling developments by casting in stone the obsolete structures that today are choking growth.

Resistance to Change

The problem of any hierarchy is that of supervision and the losses resulting from the "agency" problem. People's tendency to pursue their own interests, to the detriment of those of the organization, means that the monitoring exerted by the manager on each employee is essential to the survival of the productive team[23].

Under these conditions it is important to ensure that the manager's orders will be correctly transmitted and carried out well. That implies tight conformism on behalf of the members of the organization: "vertical" loyalty, which consists in accurately transmitting the orders come from above and to implement them as precisely and scrupulously as possible, is essential[24].

The logic of politically correct thinking (la pensée unique). To be effective, the hierarchy also calls for a single strategy, coming from the top, and finally the existence of a single line of thought within the organization. When the leader has made his decision among all the choices that were possible, everyone must know it and implement it.

The inescapable counterparts of this operating mode, indispensable to hierarchies, are a certain slowness in designing and changing products and strategies, a certain particularism in relation to the environment, and an essential obstinacy: one cannot change production from one moment to another, it is necessary to persevere until the possible error has become absolutely manifest.

In generalizing across all the structures of organization existing within a nation, it follows that change is all the more difficult to conceive and accept when the society is strongly hierarchical. This is why, for example, France shows a notable delay compared to the United States in the practical use of computers, whereas it is often on the cutting edge of technical and administrative innovation and while international products of the most recent technology are immediately available, as everywhere else in the world.

The fact is that our civil servants chose to equip the whole country with a single original and advanced network. That gave us the Minitel before everyone else, but at the same time locked us into a stand-alone system, detached from the use of computers and modems that are the rule everywhere else. And it is only very recently, in the summer of 1997, that the government finally acknowledged the error and sought to break through the wall: "Lionel Jospin Wants to Connect the Minitel to the Internet," announces the *Tribune* (August 26, 1997).

In an article on European delays in the information and knowledge industries, *The Economist*[25] blames the omnipresent state intervention of the continental governments. Instead of having Colbertism facilitate the adoption of high technologies to the industrial practice, it actually sterilizes its adoption. Thus in spite of its high quality universities, its technical prowess and its cultural wealth, Europe is falling farther and farther behind with regard to computers, television and communication, lagging behind America by some ten years already.

In the bureaucratic system the adoption of a technique can proceed only from the top. That requires time, because first the reality of the problem must be recognized, then a single solution defined, then transmitted from the top to the bottom of the pyramid, and finally implemented. If, that is, it proves sufficiently adapted to the needs of the users. Or else it is necessary to wait until the acknowledgement of failure goes up to the summit and the whole process starts again, which is not unlike the caricatural disadvantages of Gosplan in the formerly completely hierarchically arranged Soviet system of production.

However, if all the decisions go toward the top, it is crucial to know which top priority the manager is pursuing—his personal advantage and whim, or the interest of the principals, owners or voters. The less closely controlled he is, the more he will neglect the latter. That is usually the case in very large hierarchies whose production is diversified and complex and whose control consequently requires considerable time and resources. Thus the Soviet Union could function effectively only under an iron dictatorship, that of Lenin and then of Stalin. The easing of its police system was fatal to government control of society.

In a managerial social system, in fact, the manager's arbitrary preferences direct all the production of the hierarchical apparatus. It will follow that, vis-à-vis changes of the economic environment, his choices may diverge appreciably from the voter's and consumer's choices, and that he can easily maintain his strategy unchanged, without taking account of the desires of the others.

This is in total contrast with the market mechanism by which each one chooses the goods and equipment that are appropriate to him, in the best configuration, without waiting for a central directive to reveal or legitimate his own needs. Evolution goes on then from day to day and with no delay.

Thus, market systems respond faster and do not systematically defend the decisions previously made, contrary to the tendency of managerial hierarchies. Those have difficulty in reforming for it is the management who must decide, from the top, to question themselves and to act to some extent against themselves, whereas they are sovereign and escape from external pressures. And the difficulty is felt in particular during times of crisis where rapid and radical mutations are necessary.

We are seeing the consequences of this today: the economy has performed poorly for several years in France and Germany. In Japan, where the deceleration is spectacular, the financial system, which is in the hand of the Ministry of Finances, is quasi-bankrupt. These highly hierarchical countries can grow quickly when the wind is favorable, but they have trouble "to trim the sails" and to maneuver effectively when the wind is contrary.

Two Cultures. Countries with reduced hierarchies and more developed markets, on the contrary, can better adapt. Thus British-Colombia, alone among the states of Canada, was able to play a groundbreaking role in the privatization process, in the Seventies, whereas at the same moment the federal government was increasing the scope of the welfare state. That could not have happened in a country with a more concentrated administrative hierarchy.

There is certainly never permanent and integral stoppage in strongly hierarchical societies that, nevertheless, leave a broad segment of their production to the activity of competitive firms and markets. Western Europe is not the Soviet Union, in spite of its high degree of hierarchization. But change comes slowly and with difficulty there, in an era of a rapidly changing environment.

This natural rigidity of hierarchies is further reinforced by the anti-economic, anti-market ideology and bent of the members of the organization. From Williamson's point of view, the market is indeed the rival of the hierarchical system of production. One often assimilates market economics and corporations, whereas actually they are two competing modes of production, one centralized and the other decentralized. A perfectly competitive market would be an example of extreme decentralization. On this "atomistic" market, each firm exerts only an infinitesimal influence because it is reduced to minimal size, that of the craftsman's industry.

However, most members of an organization participate on a more or less daily basis in a culture that is hierarchical, therefore centralized, whose principles are opposed to those of the market. Labor relations are vertical between superiors and subordinates, whereas they are horizontal in markets, where competitors have equal status. Subservience to orders and adherence to the company line (politically correct thinking) are the rule in hierarchies, whereas autonomy and the individual search for original and competitive ideas are essential to anyone who wishes to survive in the market.

The culture, the "wiring," of civil servants belonging to public or private organizations is thus completely opposed to that which is promoted by the play of the market. Those who are closest to the market culture in hierarchical organizations are the salesmen, who spend their lives in contact with customers and competitors and not wrapped up in the accepted train of thought of the company pyramid. But these are also the people whose prestige is weakest in a managerial society.

The anti-economic ideology and the economic ignorance which play such an important role in French society[26] only reflect the dominating role of the hierarchical organizations and their strong concentration in our country. The fact that the French continue to pin their hopes on a career in the civil service, while at the same time they complain about the state (according to a recent survey in *Le Figaro* of April 5, 1997) is proof of an ideological recognition of the realities of organization. The public sector continues to augment its appropriations, expressed as a percentage of the national product, whereas overall growth is wavering. It is better under these conditions to belong to a large bureaucratic organization than to be a salesman out in the markets.

The preponderance of the anti-market ideology in our society means that responsibility for the least economic difficulty is generally blamed on the markets, those scabrous sources of all evil, while at the same time the real source of the problem lies in the overblown hierarchies that choke growth.

The approach is not new. The school of the "moralist economists," of Karl Polanyi, George Lefebvre, Barrington Moore and Charles Tilly, interprets for example the peasant revolts which preceded the French Revolution as so many protests against the irruption of the markets in traditional rural society. It made the fate of the peasants more precarious and reduced the quality of their lives.

But there is a confusion, as shown by Hilton L. Root[27], between protests against the monopolization of the markets by noblemen converted to businessmen, leaving to the farming community only the congruent portion of revenue from the exchanges, and the development of freely functioning markets which offered the peasants new opportunities for prosperity, of which they were heartily disposed to avail themselves. The correctly interpreted peasant protest targeted in fact those who distorted the development of competitive markets and prevented them from benefiting fully from it, which is quite a different matter.

In the same way today, the anti-economic ideology that still dominates Europe deplores the fact that international trade and the societal shifts which it entails are impoverishing employees. But it is the tax on labor, which is used to finance vast bureaucracies, and the policy of revaluation of the exchange rate (which is the doing of the euro-statists), that are responsible for unemployment.

But in the hierarchical culture, the market is always the designated scapegoat. Under these conditions the reforms that are required, if we are to benefit fully from the new opportunities offered by the global dynamics of the markets, will be refused. They will end up being accepted only at the last moment and grudgingly, at that, in the implementation of tardy reforms, "staggered change," instead of evolving continuously, "in real time," to use a common expression from the communication industry.

Staggered Reform

Since hierarchical organizations tend to be conservative, reforms take a long time. Their need must reach a certain magnitude to come to the attention of the leader at the apex of the pyramid. Studying them also requires time. Implementing centralized change is likely to upset and to diminish the ensemble's operation in unknown—that is, high-risk—ways. Moreover, the person holding the power will be naturally reticent to reduce it if, for example, the change calls for a less centralized structure.

He generally prefers to carry out authoritative "reforms," "top-down," or "purges" in the case of the Soviet Union. Those have a double advantage indeed: they make certain to pass along the instruction of the change of strategy, but at the same time they allow the leader to be periodically ensured of his subordinates' fidelity in the transmission of his orders to the bottom of the ladder. Purges dissolve the parasitic relations and horizontal interferences that are born from a too great familiarity, and the collusion that results from it, between colleagues of the same hierarchical level. It acts, in fact, to restore the leader's power to control, that is, to reaffirm the hierarchically arranged character of the organization.

The importance of State hierarchies in society makes reform more difficult still. In a private money-making firm, pressure from the shareholders, exerted freely and at low cost on the financial markets, can oblige management to restructure, to refocus, and to reduce the number of hierarchical levels. In the hierarchical political society, by contrast, the mechanisms of democratic control are less expeditious, slower, more difficult because of the rational ignorance of the voter. It also takes more time before the source of the failures is clearly identified.

In the interval, the omnipresent and quasi-monopolistic propaganda of technostructure (the "microcosm"), or the ideology of "the moralist economy," which poses the state as the best defender of individuals against the rapacity of the markets, rules the day. It is diffused permanently by the centralizing power and delays the awakening of the need for adapting to new circumstances.

In the case of the USSR, extreme it is true, it was necessary to wait for the total collapse of the economy and the society before change could occur. In the less hierarchical economies of continental Europe it will be possible to avoid such a disaster, but the reform movement remains very slow, contrary to that which happens in the more decentralized and "horizontal" societies of the United States and Great Britain.

Within the framework of a very great state, the future is approached reluctantly, adjustments are made unwillingly, and as often as possible by moving in the wrong direction. When, after long resistance, the leadership finally launches reforms that allow the free play of competitive markets, public opinion, having been endlessly warned against the dangers of such solutions, no longer understands. Events that actually constitute progress are interpreted as so many defeats.

Lack of comprehension engenders weakness. The contradiction

between the ambient ideology and the realities is too strong. The systematic demoralization of "market rivals" by the employees protected by the great hierarchies causes a feeling of injustice and impotence. The debate is obscured, the misinterpretations are continuous. Essential and beneficial reforms are disguised as so many steps backward, which is true only for the administrative class, whose domain and privileges are called into question, while the average citizen, on the contrary, will benefit from the change. There is a "social rift" between the political managers and the employee-voters. A syndrome of collective depression follows.

The same sort of phenomenon even more deeply affected the so-called people's democracies under Soviet occupation, as well as the USSR before 1989, swamping in its wake the discouraged population, as manifested in absenteeism and half-hearted labor, alcoholism and delinquency.

In the democracies of Western Europe change is occurring, despite everything that stands in the way. However, there are notable differences, according to the degree of managerialism and hierarchization. France constitutes the extreme case of the European problem.

French capitalism is managerial capitalism of a banking type but, by comparison with Germany, a strong state's role further reduces the incentives for restructuring. That is why a good number of large French companies in the public sector underwent catastrophic losses without the shareholders appearing to worry about it overmuch, and without their taking major sanctions against their management.

On the contrary, the attitude in official circles remains very favorable to managerialism—for example it condemns takeover bids, which are the definitive means to oblige managers to produce efficiently, while public opinion, influenced by the trade unions and the media, sees any restructuring of the public sector as a move directed against the users.

France's extreme managerialism leads thus many authors, fully apprised of Tocqueville's analysis, from Alain Peyrefitte (*Le Mal fran-çais*) to Michel Crozier, to take up the title of the latter's best-known work and diagnose it as a "sclerotic society." Conservatism would seem to prevent any wide-ranging change, would indefinitely maintain obsolete pre-modern structures, until the environmental pressure causes an explosion at the front of the stage, setting the scene for a political and social revolution.

This analysis was recently disputed by Ezra Suleiman, a political scientist at Princeton and a top expert on our meritocratic system[28]. According to him, the sclerotic society is only a complacently entertained myth and the reality, on the contrary, is that of continuous and successful change. And he describes the remarkable growth of an economy judiciously guided by the state, as well as the stability of a political world that has been able to adapt within the framework of a democratic and flexible constitution at the same time. The author, who is a specialist in this question, is known for usually being rather more critical[29]. He denounces, of course, the excessive elitism that fosters an "aristocracy in democracy," or the "republic of the civil servants." But on the whole, everything is for the best and while one may worry about the corruption that touches politics as it does corporations, we should conclude, Suleiman says, that this phenomenon does not tarnish the excellence of the French society. Why haven't there been taxpayers' revolts in France as one sees regularly in the United States? Because the state is well managed. And aren't the exceptional stability as well as the monopoly power of our elites alarming? Where any economist immediately sees the inefficiency of the government apparatus and the extortion of rents from the citizens and taxpayers, Suleiman distinguishes only the continuation of a French cultural tradition whose longevity justifies the maintenance, and the excellence, of the recruitment of civil servants who inevitably protect us from worrying about "wild" markets since they call into question the influence of the hierarchies.

Admittedly, he is partially right when he notes that France was able to change, mainly in the area of the economy. This is especially the case with private, competitive firms, which contrast with the public sector debacles that have been coming to the surface since the beginning of the decade. But this dynamic does not negate the thesis of the sclerotic society, belonging to the sphere of political and bureaucratic power, to the closed and self-reinforcing club of "public-private" managers who govern us, sometimes in the administration, sometimes in politics, and just as easily at the head of large companies, private or public. It is the "nobility of state" which Pierre Bourdieu exhaustively describes[30].

In this society, reform comes late and is suppressed, and inevitably causes abrupt jolts because it is not explained reasonably to the public and becomes on the contrary the object of an intense counter-propaganda in the spirit of the etatist ideology of "the moral economy." Alas, the reforms are always made essential by the condemnable but irresistible force of the international markets and the Anglo-Saxon speculators.

France is thus not truly a sclerotic society. It is a society that changes but which is in permanent crisis, because its elites are rigid, monopolist and anti-economic. They deny the value of the solutions that they end up adopting. This inconsistency makes the social development incomprehensible: the psychological principle of search for coherence is ridiculed. That explains the "seduction of pessimism" and the "collective depression" referred to by Suleiman.

Examples of reforms imposed from the top have not been lacking in the past twenty years. Let us briefly note some of the most revealing.

The first example is that of national champions and huge national investment projects. Here we have a case of exacerbated Colbertism from the end of the DeGaulle and Pompidou eras, prolonged by Giscard's and then Mitterrand's republics—time of great industrial projects favored by the top corps of engineers. The ideology, inherited from that of the Liberation, is that of state capitalism financed by taxes and the state-owned banks. Civil servants in the ministries are supposed to be the most capable of conceiving the best projects for industrial investment. The conjunction of the engineering spirit and the political ambition of civil servants sets in motion an exclusive pursuit of technical prowess and prestige, without consideration for economic cost or profitability. It doubles as a massive consumption of public funds in white elephant project in obsolete sectors that have the favor of those in power [31].

The apex was reached with the Concorde, which was denounced by the clear-headed thinkers of the time as economic nonsense and social favoritism, since the taxpayer's money was used to subsidize private managers, high-ranking civil servants and politicians as well as their close relations. But political power weighted in favor of the supersonic jet for reasons of prestige. With the subsequent failure which is well-known.

The second example is the nationalization program. This started at the end of the Seventies in the context of the irresistible rise of the socialist ideology and the nationalizing bent of the joint Socialist-Communist platform. In *L'Antiéconomique* (*Anti-Economics*), Jacques Attali and Marc Guillaume proclaim with immense "modesty" and exceptional (in)competence the end of economic science. The very existence of Objective or widely established economic knowledge is denied by the authors. All is political, and politics can sway anything, including decreeing the growth rate. The "so-called" economic analysis is actually used only as a veil for reactionary policies.

The ground being thus cleared, nationalizations were to constitute the "spearhead of growth." Whereas Great Britain and Canada started to launch privatization programs, France resolutely turned its back on the liberalization trend and returned to 1945, in other words, to the expedients of the war economy of 1914-1918, later adopted on a massive scale by the Russian Communists.

At the time, it was difficult to find ten economists in France who openly opposed this fundamental reversal [32].

However, the result of the "brilliant" anti-economic analysis, which garnered practically everyone's support, was easy to predict: the nationalizations of 1982 led to failure, the most costly manifestations of which would appear much later, in the Nineties. The program of massive revival through public expenditure accompanied by a bludgeoning of private companies led the economy into an impasse in just a few months.

The third example relates to the debate on retirement. From the very early Eighties, it became clear that the compulsory pay-as-you-go system was heading for very serious difficulties. This reality was quite simply denied by the civil servants, the trade unions and the politicians. Those who were looking into the problem were reproached with weakening the system by their misplaced fear-mongering, as later they were reproached for criticizing the single currency as weakening the franc by setting the scene for "international speculators." The French system of social security was considered the best in the world and, in an amazing inconsistency, the only one possible.

This admirable system consists of tapping the younger generations, who will never again see the money that they are pouring into funds lost in this barrel of Danaïdes. But it does not really matter, for the people in power: it is the price to be paid to maintain the existing institutions.

In a collective work published at the time[33], with some colleagues from various countries, we showed that the problem was the same one everywhere. The pay-as-you-go system was going to run up against severe demographic counter-trends from 2005-2015 and it was important to switch over as quickly as possible to a system that would be at least partially capitalized. That made the left and its economists howl, as well as the civil servants and right-wing politicians.

In this case again, the report ended up making an impact, and the need for a reform today is largely recognized. But resistance has not been overcome and the pay-as-you-go lobby is effectively slowing down the change. Where other countries have adopted radical reforms and passed without difficulty to individual choice and to capitalization, France still wonders about the introduction of complementary pension funds that would make it possible to safeguard the present system. Meanwhile, young people are still obliged to pay the retirement tax, which does not give them any rights for the future and amounts to an obligatory purchase of state bonds with a negative yield.

The fourth example is provided by French-style privatization of the large state-owned firms. After having tardily turned their back on the obsolete ideology of nationalization, given the results of that experiment, our public financiers decided to try privatization—but within the framework of collusionist capitalism, or capitalism without shareholders. Granted, in the pursuit of this form of privatization our public financiers consider quite out of the question the idea of giving control of large companies, and especially over their managers, to the shareholders. Consequently, the government organized a system of cross participations that leave the effective power at the top of privatized firms in the hands of managers coming from a background in public office, who are part of the club authorized to glean these privileges just like the abbots of the *Ancien Régime* who readily accepted State benefits.

The most visible result appeared, in the Nineties, in a spectacular falling apart of the largest companies from the moment when international competition became more intense and began to sanction management errors accumulated over the course of time. The pseudo-capitalist companies finally were reformed and restructured. But after having approached the brink of bankruptcy and receiving massive subsidies paid by the taxpayers.

The fifth example is monetary and social. It relates to the euro and the health system. In the second chapter we showed what was the grand plan for the single currency. In the next one we will examine the problem of social security and the health system.

Let us stress, here, only that once again the centralist and governmental solution won and dominated the thought of our elites, which in addition imposed it on public opinion. In all these cases of intellectual and political confrontation, the denouement is always identical: at first, extreme conservatism preached as the "only reasonable" analysis of the problem, if we even allow that there may be a problem. The leading elite then takes this error as far as it can go. It gives up only when everything has been tried to safeguard the existing structures, to persevere in the way that the most elementary economic common sense condemns.

Concerning the euro, this initiative consists of affirming that political decision will win out, as with the Concorde, against all economic considerations. The plan will be carried out to its term against the opinion of the economists, just like the nationalizations of 1982. But for what result and at what price?

The danger, always the same one and ever recognized, comes from the fact that each time there is only one "truth" or official thesis, without any consideration for the judgement of the independent professionals who perform the economic analysis. Once again, everything starts as political with the expectation that the economy will follow. Unfortunately, it does not work that way. And the errors that the official and centralizing culture lead to are proving increasingly expensive in a time of intense competition and global markets. Other countries are handling this better than we do, according to their greater or lesser degree of managerialism.

Germany and Great Britain

The extent of the corporate restructuring that occurred in the

United States in recent years is well-known. So much so that certain economists and financial theorists such as Michael Jensen, professor at the Harvard Business School, see it as a new industrial revolution, the third one[34]. For Jensen, the wave of mergers and acquisitions, which continues unabated throughout the country, is due to the maturing of many American industries.

The revolution of data processing and communications, genetic engineering and the reduction of optimal size of firms call for a massive restructuring to reallocate their capital and human resources for the future.

This tidal wave also touches, though to a lesser degree, the European economies. But it affects them differently, according to whether their model of organization is more or less centralized and hierarchical. The contrasted examples of Great Britain and Germany such as reported by *The Financial Times* (March 10, 1997) are very revealing of these different approaches.

During the ten last years, the wave of restructuring led to a general questioning of the strategy and organization of firms in both countries. The tendency was, as everywhere, to concentrate on the core business and to simplify the structures of internal organization, that is, to reduce the size of the staffs and to reduce the number of hierarchical levels.

But the intensity of these transformations was very unequal in British versus German firms. Cutbacks, re-specialization and the reduction of the number of hierarchical levels were much more radical in the first than in the second.

That is the conclusion of a survey from the Center for Economic Performance of the *London School of Economics,* conducted by Ansgar Richter and Geoffrey Owen, on the evolution since 1986 of the hundred and sixteen largest British and German firms. More than three-quarters of the big English companies reduced their diversification. More than half gave up certain divisions or sold off part of their product lines. And 80% of these firms turned to subcontracting.

On the other hand, the large German companies were more re-served with regard to restructuring. That may be due, partly, to their having engaged in less diversification in the Sixties and Seventies than their British homologues did. However, even giant conglomerates like Veba and Viag did not show much enthusiasm for increasing their fo-cus on their core business. In spite of criticisms from American and British financial analysts, the management of the German conglomer-ates seems to remain very confident in their capacity to manage a broad range of various activities. This attitude is characteristic of very managerial firms.

Many of the de-diversification deals in Great Britain were trans-acted through a corporate buy-out by its employees (LMBO). And nearly 60% of the large companies sold some of their activities to their top executives, whereas this type of transaction really appeared in Ger-many only since the reunification and involves only 20% of the large companies.

Along the same lines, the majority of recent acquisitions in Great Britain relate to horizontal mergers, that is, between firms in the same trade, only 16% concerning activities nondependent on the principal trade, whereas in Germany these last represent 32% of the transac-tions. In Germany, these mergers and acquisitions are also much more frequently geared toward vertical integration, for example in the case of manufacturers purchasing a distributor.

These two countries' firms also differ in their policy on interna-tional acquisitions. Almost 50% of British acquisitions aim at foreign targets, to which we can add 20% of transactions aimed equally at both foreign and British companies. In Germany, by contrast, interna-tional acquisitions represent only 31% of the transactions while the proportion of geographically diversified transactions is stronger (36%).

Nevertheless, the tendency to decentralize management is similar in the two countries, the financial decisions for example being more and more often entrusted to the operational managers. In the same way the tendency to reduce the number of hierarchical levels is identical in both countries. Ten years ago, there was an average of 7 levels in Great Britain, and it could reach 14 in extreme cases. This has dropped to 5 in 1996, thus decreasing by a third. In Germany, on the basis of a lower initial level of 5 to 6 hierarchical echelons in 1986, the firms also tended to reduce the number in 1996.

Altogether, German firms were much more timid in their approach to restructuring than British firms. Probably the system of financing through banks, and the cross shareholdings, provided fewer incentives to change than the open and impersonal system of financing through the financial market.

From this point of view, there are many observers who have long been predicting the opening of Germany's closed system of financing. Until now nothing has happened. But perhaps we are on the eve of an evolution. The new President of Deutsche Bank AG, the largest financial establishment beyond the Rhine, has just informed his compatriots that they should prepare for a new kind of capitalism, which would involve buy-outs, hostile as well as friendly [35]. This has implications for the competitiveness of the economy and brings a new era for German capitalism. Rolf Breuer wants to develop the activities of German commercial banks while turning away from the tradition by which its top executives sit on the boards of directors of the firms where it holds a share of the capital.

This statement comes just a short while after Deutsche Bank advised the steelmaker Krupp Hoechst AG in its hostile tender offer for rival steelworks, Thyssen AG, which drew sharp reactions from the trade unions, traditional partners of the club of managers.

CONCLUSION

The economic of organization shows that the Super State would come as an addition on top of the hierarchical structures existing in the continent. Thus would be created a large managerial and corporatist capitalist country, relatively closed to the outside, that would not favor reform of the productive and administrative structures.

However, such reforms are imperative in Europe, and first of all in the welfare state systems. Although, economically, we have caught up with America, the new economic challenge to which the continent must respond is to develop sufficiently strong dynamics to put us on the road to sustained high growth. That is far more difficult than implementing already known techniques and imitating a leading country. Since 1975 we have had to invent and create. The state shows little success at that: overall, the Pompidou industrial policy of the early Seventies was a failure. The Socialists' industrial policy and nationalization, to some extent prolonged by the "core group of shareholders" privatization strategy in the following years, turned disastrous in the Nineties.

We must turn to a policy and an ideology radically opposed to those of the past. That is today's challenge, more acute than ever as international competition requires enhanced efficiency. We must take a fresh look at the state redistributive processes. This time it is the state that is in question and not only the companies that depend on its subsidies. Like any commercial firm, the state must be reformed. That has not happened for more than half a century, since it had been enjoying permanent expansion.

However, small hierarchies are more easily reformed. That is what helps the small countries that are open to the outside. And most of them adopt a model of organization giving a large role to the markets. Major reforms have taken place in recent years in New Zealand, the Netherlands, in Canada. They do not depend on traditional political loyalties and have been led by socialist governments as well of as by governments on the right.

In the larger, more managerial countries, the task appears more difficult, given the longer latency period for policy change and the more timid approach to reform.

This is why the Super State would constitute a paralyzing superstructure that would further hobble the movement toward change. Being a cartel of national states with huge potential power, it would reduce the competition between them and increase the hierarchization of European societies. Collectively, they constitute an economy that is relatively less open to the outside than are those of the individual member states, and much more inclined to a conservatism which the monetary policy of the euro only partially prefigures.

By standing as an obstacle to necessary change, the European political superstructure, contrary to the present needs, is an expression of hierarchical conservatism that will choke off future growth.

Chapter IV

SO, HOW DO WE
GET OUT OF THIS?

The construction of the Very Great State, the first stage of which consists of creating a single currency, locks us into the trap of a conservative macroeconomic program characterized by the sterilizing course of a balanced budget. To get out of this dead end requires, first of all, a return to a realistic monetary policy, that essential condition of recovery. Recovery will follow quickly as it did in several countries that chose this strategy.

As growth finds its normal rate, it will then be possible to look at the true problem of European societies at the end of the century, that of tax and social reform.

The welfare states, designed more than fifty years ago to provide a complement of resources to the less favored for rather short periods of retirement as well as a basic, limited protection against the risk of disease, became immense machines for the redistribution of a fifth or even a quarter of the national income. They now provide a principal income during long years of retirement to the entire population, as well as comprehensive insurance in the event of disease.

The very objective of the system was lost from sight, given that the effects of the tax on labor, which finances it, are more and more heavily felt on the labor market. A good part of the increase in the rate of "natural" unemployment is explained thus by the continual growth of social taxes.

The magnitude of these systems and the participation of the most powerful social groups in their management naturally make it difficult to reform them. The simple effort to limit the administrative staff without changing the whole apparatus has failed everywhere. It is, however, possible to imagine passing the control to the insured themselves, safeguarding at the same time the income redistribution component in favor of the most modest wages—which is the principal justification of the public intervention in this field.

This is the price to be paid to get out of the quicksand that Europe is in.

THE TRAP OF FISCAL CONSERVATISM

The economic deceleration in recent years was accompanied, as is always the case, by an imbalance of public finances. Budget deficits have increased in strong proportions and the national debt has grown heavier, expressed as a percentage of the national product, aggravated further by the tax crisis experienced by the nation-States that are more open to the outside.

Reversing the order of the factors, the thesis of budgetary conservatism, which finds particularly favorable response from the European central banks and monetary fundamentalists, would have the public deficits bear the responsibility for the modest economic growth. However, is is the tax rates, already so high in Europe that it hardly appears possible to further increase them, that should be taken into account for the rapidly growing social costs that they entail.

Indeed taxes, whatever their basis, introduced a gap, a "tax wedge," between the cost to the purchaser of the good or service considered, and what the supplier receives. By increasing the cost, including taxes, and by reducing the net price going to the producer, public levies induce a reduction of both consumption and production. This lost production purely and simply disappears from the economy. The loss of the corresponding incomes, which have vanished, constitutes the social loss resulting from the tax, or the "social cost" of the tax.

A higher tax rate thus lowers the level of national production. This loss of production increases very palpably with the rates of taxation, which explains the leveling off trend of the global rates of taxation in the Nineties. From this point on, the losses of social wealth induced by even higher taxes would be unbearable compared to the hoped-for benefit from additional public spending.

However, according to conservative budgetary analysis, today's national debt will have to be translated into increased taxes tomorrow, especially since as the receipts of privatization were essentially garnered. The only other possibility would be to resort, at the proper time, to money creation to refund the loans fallen due, which would threaten future price stability. Therefore, it would be important to reduce the deficits now while preserving the current monetary policy, and growth and employment will naturally follow.

All that sounds like common sense and falls under the old tradition of conservative management of public finances. But a slightly more precise examination of these proposals quickly exposes their weakness and arbitrariness.

During the last two decades many States had the unusual experience of sizable budget deficits during peace time. These deficits resulted essentially from increases in social expenditures, not compensated by comparable tax receipts. And these tendencies were accentuated by the decelerating growth of the Seventies and Eighties.

For most of the 20th century, the governments of industrialized countries set up and developed social programs whose increasing costs engendered the recent budgetary difficulties. While the ratio of the national debt to the national product continually went down or at least remained stable after the Second World War, partly because of unanticipated inflation and the strong growth of the economies, since 1980 the ratios of national debt to national product were everywhere trending upward.

The increase in public spending results for the most part from the massive development of the "welfare state," and in particular from the health care expenditures directly charged to the public sector or reimbursed by a public insurer, from public financing of retirement, and to a lesser extent from transfers to the poorest.

Although the mandatory deductions went up steeply, they could not keep up with the growth rate of public spending, and the debt increased considerably. This tends to prove that taxation had reached a certain limit.

Until the middle of the century, management standards for public finances called for deviating from the balanced budget only in exceptional circumstances. And in fact the public budgets were kept in balance except during the two world wars and the Great Depression of the Thirties.

But simply reporting a change in the balance of public finances does not establish the need for returning to the prior situation. Indeed, nothing proves that deficits are a major disadvantage or slow down the creation of wealth.

First of all, there is neither convincing theory nor empirical proof that budget deficits or the national debt could exert negative effects on a country's growth or level of wealth. On the contrary, it is known that debt is useful and is economically justified.

The analogy with a consumer or a one-man business makes this easy to understand. Their revenue streams do necessarily correspond to their desired spending profile. There may be greater expenditures than revenues during certain times; the converse may be true at other times. In this case, a loan makes it possible to obtain the desired profile of investment or consumer spending, independently of the temporal distribution of revenues. Debt improves the consumer's or the firm's economic situation instead of diminishing it. Nobody would claim that a zero-loan policy in all circumstances would constitute the best financial policy for either households or firms.

The same applies to States. Certain expenditures come up punctually and sometimes on a large scale. An example would be military spending in the event of war. But that is also true for social spending which increases appreciably during times of recession. The national income and consequently the "normal" tax receipts, with an unchanged rate of taxation, do not increase proportionately during these specific times. As a consequence, it would be necessary to increase the tax rates very sharply to finance the temporary increase in expenditure. That would create massive and disproportionate social losses. For Robert Barro, who proposed this analysis, debt is used for "smoothing out" the tax rates over time, which in the end increases the community's wellbeing.

It follows that loans and thus deficits can be useful if the expenditure that it finances is considered judicious.

But the precise definition of a "good" level of deficit, for a household, a firm, or a State, at the moment defies economists' analytical capacities.

Some theoretical works try to show that there is a level of deficit and debt likely to support maximum growth. But we do not know what, in practice, these levels could be. We note for the moment that economic growth can be strong with a significant public debt, as well as with a very low debt. The high growth years of the post-war period, for example, were years when States' debt level was extremely high, far higher than it is today.

Can the current growth continue for long? Nothing indicates that today's deficits are insupportable. There is certainly an arithmetic of debt that shows that beyond a certain rate of increase and beyond a threshold expressed as a percentage in the national product, an imprudent State would have to borrow more and more, simply to pay the interests on its former loans. Bankruptcy, "default" on the part of the borrower, then becomes a real possibility. But we, in Europe, are very far from such a situation. And comfortable margins remain for public loans.

In addition, it is not true that today's loan necessarily means higher taxes tomorrow or the day after tomorrow. Indeed, given a certain tax rate, stronger growth of the national product enlarges the tax base and brings in more revenue for the public finances. The ability to settle loans then increases without it being necessary to increase the tax burden.

Thus the United States, where a true hysteria about budget deficits reigned at the beginning of the Eighties and where the national debt was considered catastrophic and supposedly beyond any control, returned to very low levels of deficit today, while appreciably reducing the volume of its debt. Since 1990 the deficit was brought down from 3.2% to 1.2% of the GDP, for the simple reason that growth there was vigorous since the beginning of the decade. It is growth that made it possible to regulate the deficit problem and not the reduction of the deficit that made it possible to achieve growth.

Certainly, the majority of European countries today are in a similar situation. Deficits and debt present no real threat except, perhaps, in Belgium, Greece and Italy. Still, it should be mentioned that levels of debt higher than the national product have been reached in the past at the end of wars and that even these debts ended up being repaid.

As far as we know today, neither is it well-founded to claim that the reduction of deficits is a recipe for growth. Changing deficit levels can stimulate or slow down the expansion under way and over the medium term. That depends on several factors that complicate the analysis.

Deficit reduction can indeed come from a reduction in spending or from an increase in tax receipts, or both at the same time. In itself, spending reduction involves a Keynesian braking of aggregate demand since the deficit consists of putting into circulation more buying power than the State takes away through taxes. A reduction in the deficit consequently reduces the global demand, which affects businesses and household income. It reduces production. This effect will be even clearer if the reduction of the deficit is obtained mainly through an increase in taxation.

Thus in 1995-1996, the tax levies (on an already sluggish economy) of additional 125 billion francs plus a 25 billion increase in local taxes, caused a drain of almost 2% of the GDP, clearly exerting a strong deflationary influence on business activity and employment. And the deceleration that followed in 1996 and 1997 contributed to reducing tax receipts and to increasing social spending, as always happens during phases of slow growth and recession that increase deficits. It is the trap of budgetary conservatism, or the vicious circle of "budgetarism," which in this case has the result of aggravating the very problems that it claims to solve. In a period of difficult economic conditions, the voluntary reduction of deficit slows down growth, which in return exacerbates the deficit.

In a study of the OECD countries, Alberto Alesina and Roberto Perotti[1] show clearly that the countries that reduce their deficits by increasing taxes do not achieve a long term improvement in the balance of public finances, and in fact they experience a braking of economic activity.

Conversely, those who reduce deficits by reducing public spending without increasing taxes, or even with a reduction in household taxation, improve their financial balance lastingly and they benefit from accelerated growth. Especially if the reduction of expenditure relates to the expenditure for social security and the wages of civil servants, the two items which weigh most heavily on the dynamics of public expenditure, rather than on investment.

One may even consider a reduction of deficits accompanied by a tax cut, the reduction in spending being greater than the reduction of the deficit. In this case, the growth would be higher, the decline in taxation bringing about an increase in household wealth which translates into additional consumption.

However, all these conclusions are affected by the initial conditions of the economy. In the short term and in an economy in recession or deceleration, the tax relief would have to be substantial to compensate for the Keynesian contraction of a reduction of the deficit. Returning toward a balanced budget by reducing public investments and increasing taxation can even provoke a depression.

Lastly, the impact of deficits on growth not being necessarily positive or significant, the effect on unemployment will also be variable— and possibly opposite to that which some budgetary conservatives expect.

If one holds absolutely to reducing the deficit, it is better to do it during times of strong growth, by reducing the social security spending and trying to reduce taxes at the same time. During times of weak growth, one must be satisfied with reducing taxes to increase household wealth and to stimulate renewed consumption and investment, while accepting a temporary increase in the deficit.

The Balladur government's experiment with budgetary stimulation through deficit increases in 1994, within sight of the 1995 presidential elections, was convincing, and accelerated growth as the theory suggests it would. Its principal disadvantage has to do with the fact that this expansionist policy, correct in itself, because of the weakness of the economic activity, resulted not so much from a reduction in taxes as from an increase in public spending—quite futile given the high percentage of the national revenue that these last already represented. But especially, the still strongly restrictive monetary policy which accompanied it prevented any long lasting correction to the economy, which made impossible the stabilization and thus the automatic recovery of the public finances. It thus led to a new policy of deficit reduction, which broke the recovery once more in 1995-1996.

Thus, deficit reduction does not necessarily constitute good macroeconomic policy. It depends on the way in which it is conducted and the phase of the economic cycle in which it takes place. Its effectiveness depends in particular on the monetary policy that is pursued simultaneously.

All things considered, one cannot be satisfied with a simplistic and rigid view of what should be done in regard to budget deficits.

To affirm, then, that within the framework of a restrictive monetary policy, reducing public deficits is sufficient to restore the conditions of growth is quite simply inaccurate. Budgetarist doctrines do not rest on any serious foundation.

Saying that is not the same as advocating an increase in public spending or denying that it must be reduced, above all the spending for social security. Those indeed determine the bulk of the tax increases which involve disproportionate social losses, and which particularly afflict labor. And the tax on labor is the principal item responsible for the growth of structural or "natural" unemployment that has become so significant in our economies.

It is well understood that these ever-mounting costs make the continual rise in spending increasingly unacceptable. But what we need in order to stop this rise is a major reform of the systems of public assistance and insurance, because that is where the origin of the problem lies.

Thus we need to reform, to cut social spending, to reduce the tax burden on employment and to create again a broader base of employment that will support economic growth.

It is a task for the medium term because it takes time, whereas the social losses due to economic sluggishness and unemployment have reached a level that makes it impossible to wait any more. In addition, social reform and tax reform can hardly be achieved except during a phase of expansion because of the upheavals which they can induce on the labor market and the immediate, although transitory, loss of incomes that they will generate. This means that it is politically possible only during a time of economic revival, which only the adoption of a dynamic monetary policy can induce.

GOOD MONETARY POLICY

We return thus to our statement in the first chapter. Good monetary policy is what the European economies need today in order to attain vigorous growth. And national monetary independence conditions the establishment of a "tailor made" policy, designed to meet the specific needs of the economy of a given country, at a given moment. The return of long term growth consequently depends on an end to euro-monetarism.

The recent rise of the dollar vis-à-vis the mark and the franc is a striking illustration of the effectiveness and the powerful role of exchange rates and interest rates on the real economic — activity contrary to everything that the fundamentalists maintain. All the observers greeted the rise of the dollar as the promise of oxygen to the suffocating economies of France and Germany.

What they do not say, of course, is that the strong dollar actually corresponds to a relative weakening of the mark, and thus of the franc.

The experiment in progress on the exchange market thus shows that recovery of the continental economies results directly from the depreciation of the mark and the franc. A heresy for the proponents of the mark-standard and the strong euro! Then the best exchange rate for the economy would not be necessarily the highest.

What Exchange Rate for Growth?

A new monetary policy must put an end to the overvaluation of the franc. That can be done with or without the mark. In the first case, the depreciation would be carried out with respect to all currencies except the mark, which will follow the franc in its fall and along the same proportions. In the second, it will apply to all currencies, including the mark.

The first case means simultaneous devaluation of the mark and the franc against the dollar, the parity between franc and mark remaining unchanged. In the second, the franc would depreciate identically compared to the mark and the dollar, while the mark remains unchanged in its parity against the dollar.

Between these two extreme solutions, there is a whole range of possible depreciation rates for the franc with respect to the dollar and mark, this last by, presumably, not completely following the franc's fall compared to the American currency. The mark would then be appreciated against the franc.

How shall we evaluate the desirable "matrix" of exchange rates of the franc in relation to these two great currencies? How can we define good monetary policy and good exchange rates?

A first approach consists in seeking the parity that would engender a trade balance. One may note, as did Jean-Pierre Vesperini[2], that the last time the trade balance was in equilibrium between the United States on one side and France and Germany on the other was in 1990. If we consider that there is a shift of approximately one year in the influence of the exchange rates on the flow of international trade, we can conclude that the 1989 export prices were equilibrium prices, and that consequently the exchange rate was so also in equilibrium.

Over the five years preceding 1995 (the last statistic available), the export prices of the United States compared to those of Germany and of France dropped exactly in the same proportions, that is about 24%

compared to the base of 1989.

If we take the case of maintaining the franc-mark parity, then to restore the relative competitive position of France and Germany compared to the United States, and to bring it back to its 1989 level, would require that the dollar be appreciated in the same proportions.

Taking the dollar's average rate of exchange against the franc and the mark, observed over the year (4.99 francs and 1.43 marks per dollar), that would give an equilibrium exchange rate of approximately 6.50 francs and 1.90 marks to a dollar in 1995.

If you suppose that French and German competitiveness has not deteriorated since this date, it should be noted that even the recent appreciation of the dollar which went as far as 6.20 francs, was not enough to restore the trade balance.

Assuming an adjustment of the franc alone compared to the dollar, with the mark remaining in fixed parity with respect to the American currency (its average recent level of 1.55 marks to the dollar), the mark would have to go to 4.19 or 4.20 francs instead of the usual 3.37 or 3.38.

The unilateral adjustment of the franc's exchange rate against the dollar would involve *ipso facto* a depreciation of the franc with regard to the mark, which would consequently penalize the German economy. It thus constitutes a way to put pressure on the Bundesbank to encourage it to change its policy with respect to the dollar. If the latter agreed to follow the movement, there would be a combination of a depreciation of the franc compared to the mark and of a depreciation of the mark compared to the dollar. The precise level of these two variations would be the result of negotiation with the German government.

From this point of view, the proportions in which these two adjustments could be carried out cannot be foretold since they would rise from a political negotiation whose outcomes are uncertain.

The various solutions, however, have very different consequences for growth. If the two limiting assumptions are retained, the variations of parities bringing the dollar to 6.50 francs would produce a supplementary growth in the French GDP of 1.6% in the case of a mark remaining at 3.38 francs, while it would reach 3.6% if the mark went to 4.19 francs.

In an unchanged internal and international environment, the French economy thus would profit more from a unilateral exchange rate decision along the lines of those taken respectively by Great Britain and Italy at the time of the 1992-1993 crisis.

But one may also wonder if there is not a franc-mark parity that would stand out more than another based on broader considerations than simple equilibrium of the balance of trade at a given moment. Assessments of equilibrium exchange rates often refer to the condition known as "purchasing power parity" between two countries.

The principle here is simple. In an open and competitive international economy, the same product must be sold everywhere at the same price. Expressed in francs in Paris, it must be equal, after converting the francs into dollars at the current rate, to the price expressed in dollars in New York. Or else importers and exporters will take advantage of these differences, which will end up equalizing indeed the prices in France and the United States. The tendency toward price convergence, or the "law" of the single price, will be proven.

The Big Mac Standard and the Purchasing Power Parity

This is the principle that inspires the calculation of "the Big Mac standard" invented and presented by the weekly magazine *The Economist* for more than a decade. For McDonald's Big Mac, which is strictly identical in every country where it is sold, the price in local currency in an unspecified country, corrected for the rate of exchange in francs or in dollars of the currency considered, should be equal to the price at which it is sold for francs in Paris or for dollars in New York.

Actually this equivalency, which corresponds to the "purchasing power parity," a condition according to which the rates of exchange are adjusted to equalize the prices of the same product everywhere in the world, is generally not observed in the Big Mac index.

That is because the exchange rates chosen by the monetary authorities do not correspond to the natural balance of the economies. It is then possible to calculate what should be the exchange rate of the dollar compared to the franc so that the price of the famous sandwich would be exactly the same whether expressed in dollars or in francs, in Paris and in New York. This theoretical rate of exchange is that of the purchasing power parity.

Compared to the current exchange rate observed on the market, it gives an indication of one currency's overvaluation or undervaluation compared to another. These are these figures that we present below. In April 1997, even when it reached 5.76 francs, the dollar remained undervalued compared to the franc, or the latter was overvalued compared to the dollar.

Generally all the European currencies and in particular those dependent on the mark were significantly overvalued compared to the dollar: Belgium +28%, France +26%, Denmark +63%, the Netherlands and Austria +17% and Germany +18%.

These differences in overvaluation also give an indication of the relationships of the various European currencies to each other.

Thus within Europe, the franc appears overvalued compared to the mark, the guilder and the schilling, not to mention the countries which adopted a monetary policy independent of Germany, such as Great Britain and Italy, until recently. The gap compared to the pound sterling, which has recently been trending upward, is +4% and, compared to the lira, +13%.

There follows an unquestionable competitive disadvantage for

France, not only with regard to the United States (as is the case of all the European countries) but also compared to all its European partners including Germany, and with respect to the countries of the small mark zone, excepting only Denmark and Belgium.

This simple illustration is enough to highlight the extent of the imbalances which result from state intervention in the exchange rate, the franc being overvalued by 26% compared to the dollar, even after the appreciation of the latter at the beginning of 1997. For its part, the mark was still overvalued by 18% compared to the greenback. But it follows that the franc is also overvalued compared to the mark by some 8%.

The Big Mac standard thus gives us an approximate idea of the "ideal" matrix of exchanges, in particular between the franc, the mark and the dollar, that which corresponds to the parity of purchasing powers.

If we take the parity of the dollar that was current in 1977, that is to say approximately 5.70 francs, and apply a reduction corresponding to the percentage of overvaluation indicated by the Big Mac, we obtain a parity equilibrium ensuring the equality of purchasing power which would be around 7 francs.

As for the mark, which in 1997 was worth on average 1.67 dollars, after a depreciation of 18%, it would arrive at 1.90 dollars.

Under these conditions the equilibrium parity between the franc and the mark would be 3.65 francs for one mark instead of the current 3.36 or 3.37 francs.

If we look again at how growth in the French economy would be affected by a change in the parity with the mark and the dollar mentioned above, that would result in an increase of approximately 3.5% in the growth rate of the national product compared to the initial situation of the exchange rates.

The fall of the mark and the franc compared to the dollar that came about during the summer of 1997, the dollar reaching the exchange rate of 6.20 francs, goes part of the way back to equilibrium. But that is not enough if one refers to a parity of 7 francs to the dollar. That parity remains all the more attainable since the fall of the franc and the mark occurred without any reduction of interest rates. And there remain margins for reducing the latter.

The Impact of Zero Interest Rates

Interest rates exert a powerful impact on all economic activity through multiple channels because they act on all the major components of demand. They act on household consumption, on corporate investment, consumers' investment in housing, on the formation of inventories and exports.

This influence on growth is indisputable in theory as in practice but it is difficult to quantify very precisely. Nonetheless, the OECD offers an estimate of the incidence of a decline of the real rates by its Interlink model. These empirical analyses show that a two point reduction of the real short-term interest rates bring about a 0.5% supplement of growth of the GDP. Since these rates are currently extremely close to 2%, it would follow that bringing them back to zero would cause an additional growth of 0.5%.

That calls for two comments.

On the one hand, the short-term rates' effect on growth is less spectacular than that of the variations of exchange rates, in particular because the interest rates already fell sharply since 1993 and more particularly since 1995. Not much room for maneuver remains to stimulate growth with this instrument of monetary policy. Nevertheless, the short-term interest rates are more than 3% while inflation approaches zero. Thus there is still room for the real rates to fall three points, which is above the two points of reduction that we envisage.

In addition, it is not certain either that one can cumulate the effects which we have just distinguished: the 2% supplement of growth due to the depreciation of the exchange (the most moderate assumption), and that of 0.5% due to the fall of the short-term interest rates. Indeed, the fall of the short-term interest rates also contributes to a drop in the exchange rate as well as exerting an independent influence on consumption and investment. It is thus difficult to disentangle these two types of influence.

However, the results of the OECD make it possible to estimate cautiously as at least 2%, and perhaps 3% or more according to the various assumptions of adjustment of the exchange rates, the supplement of growth which would be induced by the new monetary policy.

If we acknowledge that in the absence of a change of monetary policy, the GDP growth rate would be 2% in 1997, this kind of change in the exchange rate and the interest rate would make it possible to attain a growth rate of approximately 4 to 5% of the GDP. It could even be slightly higher if the depreciation of the franc compared to the dollar and the mark reached that proposed on the basis of the "Big Mac" indicator.

In any event, such a large acceleration of growth would have direct consequences on employment and unemployment.

Positive Effects on Employment and Unemployment

With supplementary growth of at least 2% above spontaneous growth of the GDP (which is itself around 2%), we would obtain an effective rate of growth of at least 4%, that is to say the same as in 1989, the last year before the establishment of the monetary and exchange policy of Maastricht.

It is known in macroeconomics that the growth of production and employment are directly connected, which means that growth and unemployment are inversely connected. This is the relation known as "Okun," analyzed in the first chapter.

Thanks to some simple statistical estimates, Jean-Pierre Vesperini measures these influences. His results show clearly that in France the fluctuations of employment are strongly dependent on the variations of the GDP in the current period and the previous period. According to his estimates, if GDP growth reaches 4% a year, the number of jobs would increase by 1.4%, which corresponds to the creation of 320,000 jobs.

In addition, it has been observed that the creation of 320,000 jobs would bring down unemployment by about 170,000 people, that is to say a 0.6% reduction in the rate of unemployment in the year in question. Indeed, the variations of the rate of unemployment are equal to the variations of the working population minus the variations of employment. If we suppose that the working population increases by 150,000 people, it follows that unemployment would drop by 170,000 people because of the creation of 320,000 jobs.

This effect then would be repeated year by year as long as the parity of the exchange rate maintains growth at 4%. Three years of expansion would thus reduce by almost a half-million the number of unemployed, that is to say about half of cyclical unemployment due to France's slow growth. This is still a particularly cautious estimate, the United States and Great Britain having done much better in the same lapse of time.

In conclusion, a monetary policy for France alone would induce strong acceleration of growth and consequently an appreciable increase in job creation and a correlative reduction in unemployment.

Then there remains the problem of structural unemployment and the explosive spending of the welfare state. The return to growth makes it possible to consider structural reform, which will produce its effects over the medium term.

TAX AND SOCIAL REFORM

Social security spending (retirement and health care) constitutes the fastest growing part of all public spending. It thus explains, for the most part, the increase in mandatory withholdings during the last quarter century. The two levies that increased to a significant degree are the direct tax on income and the tax on labor. And the same statement is true of all the great economies. The outcome is that social spending is also the engine driving the employment crisis. The welfare state's spending makes the taxes go up and the latter, in the form of social contributions, introduce a "tax wedge" (or social wedge) on the labor market, which has the direct effect of destroying employment. It is, together with restrictive macroeconomic policy, the principal source of unemployment. This is what needs to be changed.

These findings are known today. For example, the recent La Martinière report on taxation states:

> For seven years France, of all the large developed countries, has been the one where the current resources of the public administrations represented the highest percentage of the gross domestic product. In our country this proportion has constantly exceeded the average observed within the G7 Member States by approximately twelve points . . .
>
> It goes without saying—although this obviousness is sometimes lost from sight—that the level of taxation is narrowly conditioned by the level of public spending. That is what makes the taxation necessary...
>
> In this respect, it hardly seems useful to stress that social expenditures, up to recent times, were characterized by a continuous heavy burden, going from 25.4% of gross domestic product in 1980 to 29.8% in 1994. Half of this development is due to the progression of health care spending...
>
> The demographic trends will necessarily entail large cost overruns in a few years. These prospects confirm that controlling health insurance costs is essential and that priority must be given to resuming growth and creating jobs, which addresses a budgetary need as much as a moral concern. (*Summary*, pp. 6-8.)

And the reporter continues:

> In every respect, income tax finds itself in a vicious circle. The high rates, burdened down over the passing years by additional levies, encourage legislators to add loopholes and exemptions, deductions and reductions. Exploited with increasing expertise, these facilities chip away at the tax and lead to decreasing returns. It is imperative to break out of this vicious circle and to start a virtuous circle: a significant drop in the rates of the tax scale should enable us to clear away the tangle of loopholes which undermine the equality of citizens and of tax neutrality . . .

> In addition, reducing the rates and widening the tax brackets could offer the additional benefit of extending the tax base and thereby providing some room for maneuver. (*Summary*, pp. 19-20.)

These conditions define very precisely the two major problems of the French tax system, the same problems that one finds everywhere else on the continent:

First, the burgeoning social security taxes, the taxes that went up most significantly in recent years, and that which most directly hurt employment;

Second, the progressive income tax that, at the other end of the wage spectrum, discourages initiative and effort.

Whereas most other countries have given up extreme marginal rates, they remain very high in France without bringing significant receipts to the State. It is known, through several foreign experiments, that punitive rates very sharply reduce the base of declared wages and incomes. So the progressive scale does not really redistribute incomes, either, since it dries up the very source of the tax.

Together, the two taxes degrade our companies' competitiveness, and at the same time penalize growth and employment. Thus, one cannot hope to find the structural conditions for sustained high growth—nor fully to profit from it if it should again become possible due to a potential change in macroeconomic policy or a more favorable international climate—until we remedy the double tax penalization which we inflict on production and employment.

This diagnosis leads to the consideration of a fundamental reform that aims to reduce both the social security taxes and the income tax rates. Of necessity, that requires a complete restructuring of the social systems which are financed by the payroll tax.

As regards retirement, the analyses are many and well-known. As a consequence, we will concentrate on reforms of the health insurance system, which seems to confront the timid attempts at modernization with such insurmountable difficulties that until now reforms have been limited to plans for administrative rationing of spending.

However this method, which does not change the economic incentives influencing the various partners of the system, inevitably dissatisfies them all. Indeed, the mechanisms in place all push in the direction of increased spending: a very complete coverage for health risks (compulsory, not chosen by tax payers), automatic payment of the premiums through the payroll tax, the absence of a profit motive or even the requirement of balancing premium receipts and disbursements for the monopolist insurer and, in addition, the doctors' natural concern for treating their patients in the best way possible, which often means in the most expensive way since the latter benefit from maximum insurance coverage.

Under these conditions the government, which arbitrarily limits the expenditures that are all under pressure to increase, has consistently inspired unanimous opposition. The pitiless and effective government rationing that each new minister announces is usually abandoned after a few months, and the cycle of tax-and-spend takes off once more.

The only way to put an end to this, and to allocate expenditures and resources in an economically and socially more efficient way, is to open the range of choice to all the interested parties by confronting them with the true prices and costs of their decisions. We must change the individual incentives for the policyholder as well as the health care provider. That requires a profound reform of the system's architecture.

A Realistic Plan

To be politically acceptable, a large-scale tax reform must adhere to a very strict list of conditions. It should impoverish neither the employees nor the State, and it should not compromise the social character of the earlier redistribution of incomes.

That leads to two apparently insoluble conundrums. How can the average and marginal income tax rates be reduced without reducing the State's receipts? In addition, how is it possible to reform the health care system, a prerequisite to reducing the social contributions, without compromising its social aspect by which the wealthiest employees currently pay a share, or all, of the health insurance costs for the lowest wage earners?

Indeed, the health taxes are proportional to wages, whereas the cost of insurance is the same for two employees who may have different incomes and present the same risk. This subsidy which the most modest wage earners enjoy allows everyone to obtain the same complete insurance coverage, and thus constitutes an aspect of the social safety net for the least well-paid.

Consequently, a realistic plan for reform must simultaneously achieve the five following goals.

1. To unbundle the tax on labor (which is what the required Medicaid contributions amount to) from the development of health care spending, while giving an incentive to policyholders to exercise some control over this expenditure and their insurance coverage;

2. To massively reduce the rate of the Medicaid tax, and consequently to reduce the companies' labor costs, which will allow for a significant increase in employment and a substantial reduction of unemployment;

3. To reduce the income tax rates for every category of employees;

4. To maintain income transfers in favor of the most modest wages, which the present health insurance system provides;

5. And all this while maintaining all paid workers' real standard of living, and the tax receipts that the State achieves through the income tax.

The proposal which follows aims to meet these objectives by greatly reducing the tax on labor, by reducing the income tax rates, while maintaining the social transfers (to those with modest wages) of the present health insurance system, and by maintaining the same opportunity for health insurance currently enjoyed by every employee, whatever his level of income.

The Plan

The general idea, initially, is to change how health insurance is obtained; it should no longer be provided automatically by the public monopoly insurer financed by the payroll tax, but should be purchased individually in the market. By making the employees directly responsible for health insurance payments, instead of withholding the premium at the source before payment of wages as is done today, take-home pay would be increased. And that makes it possible to bring down the income tax rates on wages that are increased by the reform.

Social security contributions (the tax on labor) are then used exclusively to ensure income transfer from the highest wages to the lowest wages, which today allow the latter to be subsidized for the use of health insurance. These transfers are to be maintained

One thus uncouples health care and health insurance expenses on the one hand and, on the other hand, the social security taxes which, now reduced, are no longer used to finance insurance premiums themselves but only for the redistribution of incomes intended to help the most modest employees to buy individually the obligatory health insurance.

As a consequence of this plan, take-home pay will go up, which will increase the receipts from income tax, thus enabling the State to scale down the tax schedule in order to preserve only the same amount of receipts as before. The tax paid remains unchanged but the incentive to work are improved since the percentage of increased wages paid to the state is lowered.

The solution starts from a simple proposition: the current social security withholding tax mixes up the obligatory purchase of health insurance for all employees with the redistribution of incomes between high wages and modest wages.

Indeed, in insurance, the actuarial premium is usually independent of the policyholder's income. It only depends on the level of risk covered, which generally is not a function of the level of wages when the guarantee is the same for all, which is the case with today's health coverage.

However, the social security contributions are not identical for every employee, but approximately proportional to the level of wages. As a result, high wages earners pay more than the health insurance premium, while the lower earners get the same coverage although they pay less than the true cost of the insurance. The latter are thus subsidized by the better-paid, via social security payroll tax which takes more from the former.

Let's examine this phenomenon in concrete terms. In 1993 all the insured, that is 19.4 million people, paid a total of 495,000 billion francs for health protection. In an insurance system where the people in good health pay for those who are unwell, the actuarial premium would be based on the average expenditure per policyholder, that is to say 25,000 francs a year (495,000 billion/19.4 million).

Consequently, all the social security policyholders who pay a Medicaid contribution "M" more than 25,000 francs in fact deliver a net tax of M - 25 000 francs to social security. This tax is used to subsidize all the employees who pay less than 25,000 francs for Medicaid. The latter receive 25,000 - M, M being their health insurance contribution (the payment from the employer and the payment from the employee combined).

Thus each one can easily calculate the net payment or the net subsidy which he receives from the community.

There are thus two main categories of employees, those who are net contributors to social security and those who are net beneficiaries of this solidarity. This social support system must be maintained as it is.

Under these conditions, each employee should receive as an addition to his wage the value of the health insurance premium that he currently subscribes through the labor tax; and that will make it possible to reduce the payroll tax.

These much reduced social contributions will no longer be used except to redistribute income in order to permit the net beneficiaries to obtain at lower cost the same health coverage as the wealthiest contributors, exactly as in the current system.

Each employee, whose wages thus will be augmented by the amount of the health insurance premium, will have to buy his own insurance within the framework of a legal obligation, similar to that which already exists, for example, in the context of automobile liability.

In the case of an employee who pays a net transfer (Employee B), the company will pay to him from now on (instead of to the social security system) the fraction of the contributions that corresponds only to the health insurance premium (let's say 25,000 francs). It will continue to withhold from the gross salary and will pay in to social security the difference between the current contributions over 25,000 francs, i.e. the redistributive tax.

For the employee who contributes to social security (via his company) less than the cost of the insurance (Employee A), the wages will be increased via the inclusion of this sum by his employer, to which an "indirect wage" will be added each month in the form of a social security check corresponding to the cost of the health insurance (25,000 francs minus the current contribution).

Employee A is thus, as before, subsidized via social security for the purchase of a health insurance policy identical to that of the best paid, and thus he remains able to buy exactly the same amount of insurance coverage as today, without paying more out of his pocket— the same way he is subsidized today by the taxes of redistribution (surplus social security contributions) paid by the richest employees.

But the tax on wages was considerably reduced at the same time that all take-home pay was increased by the amount of the health insurance actuarial premium, leaving everyone's real standard of living unchanged, subject to a reduction of the income tax rates which we will examine further.

The whole system, now and after the reform, is presented in a simplified way in the table, which gives an idea of the new balance of accounts for the two categories of employees, Employee A who is a net beneficiary of social transfers and Employee B who is a net contributor.

Many Advantages

The novelty of this reform lies in the fact that now everyone can select the insurer of his choice, public or private, from existing commercial or nonprofit health insurance providers. Obtaining insurance coverage can be made into a legal obligation, to be defined by Parliament, on the basis of covering the same risks as exist today.

Such a system of mandatory insurance, with competition among insurers, already exists—with car insurance, for example.

The competition thus introduced into the health insurance field should benefit the consumer by lowering the prices for a given quality of service, or by increasing the quality of service, as is the case in

Simplified Diagram of the Reform

	Employee A		Employee B	
	Before	After	Before	After
GROSS SALARY	20	20	100	100
Employers' and employees' contributions (% of gross salary)	2 (10)	0 (0)	10 (10)	4 (4)
NET SALARY	18	18 + 2 + 4 = 24	90	90 + 6 = 96
Income tax	(10 %) 1.8	2.4	(50%) 45	48
Disposable income after taxes	16.2	21.6	45	48
Real standard of living prior to reform				
Disposable income plus consumption of health care services financed by social security contributions	16.2 + 6 = 22.2	21.6	45 + 6 = 51	48
Restitution of surplus IRS receipts from employees		2.4 - 1.8 = 0.6		48 - 45 = 3
Real standard of living after reform (and after the reduction of income taxes)		22.2		51

other fields. Consumers should see their standard of living go up even more as health insurance premiums go down under the effect of competition between the insurers, public and private.

It is also possible to introduce a degree of freedom into the choice of insurance coverage for those employees who would like to accept moderate protection ("franchise") within the framework defined by the legally mandatory insurance, and in consideration of this, their policy premium would be further reduced and they could keep the difference compared to their old premium. This would result in an incentive for saving, on the insurance itself and the degree of coverage chosen as well as on the later health expenses covered by the insurance.

A Social Policy. Overall, the new system completely preserves the redistributive character of the previous social transfers, while very appreciably decreasing the tax rate via social security withholdings and simultaneously opening opportunities for individual choice that did not previously exist with regard to the extent of coverage. Policyholders will win, thanks to the increased competition between insurers, while benefiting from true incentives to save money and limit expenses.

What is more, the growth of health care spending would be uncoupled from the tax on wages. Indeed, social security contributions would not be used for anything more than to redistribute incomes between high wages and modest wages, which represents only a fraction of the current social taxes.

The possible increase in health care spending will now be reflected in the level of health insurance premiums. Policies are no longer financed by taxation but are purchased individually by the employees. And the latter are now encouraged to control better the rise of premiums and to no longer accept the permanent upward trend. It follows that the transfers (which are used as a component for paying the policy premiums) should stabilize, without requiring permanent increases in the labor tax.

The Drop in Contributions. Because of the reform one obtains a reduction in the rates of social security contributions, which go from 10% to 0 for Employee A and from 10% to 4% for Employee B.

Admittedly, in our example, the cost of labor has not decreased since the take-home pay was raised by the same amount as the reduction of the contributions. This reflects the immediate effect of the reform, before behaviors adjust and re-negotiations take hold in the labor market. But later on, the reduction in contributions will lead to a reduction in a company's overall labor cost, and the tax reduction will allow room, in most but not in all cases, for a net increase of salaries.

Alleviating Structural Unemployment. In other words, the increase in take-home pay will be slightly less than the reduction of the social security contributions, in accordance with the elasticity of the demand for labor (which appears to be considerable, in all the quantitative studies of the labor market). Thus there will be a real although moderate reduction of companies' labor cost. But because of the high price-elasticity of the demand for labor (a meager drop in the price of labor significantly increases companies' hiring), it will entail very significant creation of new jobs.

However, the fact that the rates of take-home pay will go up by less than the reduction of the social security contributions (making it possible to lower the total cost of labor for employers) is compensated—on the one hand by the reduced cost of health insurance, which results from the introduction of competition and free choice on the part of the insured—and, on the other hand, by the additional tax receipts which the State gains because of increased employment and production.

The State can then go ahead with additional reductions of social security contributions or income taxes, which easily compensate for the slight fall of take-home pays and indeed maintains the levels of real after-tax incomes from before the reform.

Income Tax. The first element of the reform, dissociating the purchase of health insurance from the redistributive tax on labor, then makes it possible to adjust the income tax. Indeed, paying to the employees the amount which formerly went to social security has the result of increasing the take-home pay, thereby enlarging the revenue base for the income tax, and we can see in the table above that this happens after the reform, from $1.8 + 45$ (or 46.8), to $2.4 + 48$ (or 50.4).

It is thus possible to maintain income tax revenues at their former level of 46.8 by handing back $(2.4 - 1.8)$ to Taxpayer A and $(48 - 45)$ to Taxpayer B. That results in a drop in the tax rates, from 10% to 7.5% for Taxpayer A ($1.8 / 24 = 7.5\%$), and from 50% to 46.8% for

Taxpayer B (45 / 96 = 46.8%).

Each employee's tax can thus be held at its earlier level (or it can be allocated differently between high wages and modest wages, within the same overall amount) while the tax rates will be lowered (across the board or selectively, according to political preferences).

On the whole, all the employees, or those who will have benefited selectively by this reduction of the tax rate, will now be able to retain a greater portion of their future additional incomes, which is a strong incentive to work more and to take initiatives in making a profit.

In our example, the average income tax rate went from 30% to 27.5%. Although in the immediate future neither of the two paid employees improves his real income since the reduction in the tax rates was compensated by an increase in the taxable income (because of integration of the health insurance premiums into take-home pay), that will not remain the case. For all the future increases in income, the tax rates will be lower than today.

In other words, the incentive to increase labor and work effort will play out in full for the future periods.

CONCLUSION

Today, the dynamic of the welfare state is beyond government control and endangers the balance of public finances. It constitutes a burden that is continually growing heavier and undoubtedly constricts employment, and probably economic growth as well. It results from perverse tax incentives that constantly stimulate spending. A major reform is both essential and urgent.

Such reform can be carried out without any risk to the existing policy of social transfers. Quite to the contrary, the policy of social redistribution of income can be dissociated from the provision of health and retirement coverage. One thus obtains the benefit of the efficiency of a competitive insurance system while continuing a social policy as generous as may be wished, better targeted than the current one to benefit the least favored, and thus more effective.

But launching a vast reform of the welfare state is possible only in an economy where growth is vigorous and jobs are abundant. The key to recovery is, above all, a new monetary policy that turns its back on the nefarious chimera of the euro. It will be all the more effective if we also move away from budgetarism, which does not rest upon any serious theoretical justification.

Balanced public finances will follow the return to growth and the tax and social reform, whereas an obstinate pursuit of budget surpluses in a slow-growth economy can only drive it into increased difficulties.

The suitable sequence of policies and the clear distinction of the various decision horizons thus play a crucial part in extricating Europe from its economic doldrums. With the plan for a single currency, this period at the end of the century opened with a major error in economic policies. It must close with the abandonment of this same plan.

Conclusions

THE DEMOCRATIC SOLUTION

The creation of the single currency, the euro, is the most serious economic error that European governments have made since the deflationary policies that transformed the stock exchange crisis of 1929 into a decade of world depression, throughout the Thirties. It will lead to a still more serious political error: the attempt to merge the nation-states of the continent into a single State of very great size.

The path toward the euro forbids member States to adopt "custom made" monetary policies that would be appropriate to the specific needs of their businesses. Aligning all national monetary administration on the most conservative model, that of Germany, causes the chronic stagnation and mass under-employment from which our economies suffer. This prohibitive cost will not be limited to the phase of establishing the euro. It will persist after its creation since it results from the single monetary policy.

The error is also political. The single currency inevitably leads to the creation of a European super-State, without which the euro is not viable. Between sovereign nations, currency cannot be shared, and there is no example, contemporary or historical, of a currency managed collectively by several States.

This is precisely what the partisans of the euro have in mind—they want to impose political unification without the consent of their fellow-citizens, through the "technical" artifice of the creation of the new currency.

But the construction of a State of continental dimension goes against all the requirements and all the tendencies of the contemporary economy. For nearly a quarter century all the large organizations, public and private, have been splitting up, breaking apart, and seeking efficiency in small size, as the example of Russia demonstrates.

A continental super-State will be not very efficient and will bring prohibitive costs through additional taxes that will be added to the existing national taxes. It will not improve the public services in Europe. Conversely, by abolishing competition between national States, it will paralyze the reform of old structures that are slowing down growth throughout the continent.

A useful Europe, that of the large market and competition between businesses and States, has already been created. To try to top it off with a single State is to destroy its virtues and to derail its long-term expansion.

Why then, faced with such a sobering balance-sheet, has the European error been obstinately pursued for ten years? One cannot avoid raising questions, in the face of an undertaking carried out with such determination, against the most elementary economic common sense.

*

The responsibility is clearly that of the Franco-German couple. The plan for Europe is the expression of the agreement between the two countries. The German leadership agreed to it, often against their public opinion, provided that the euro is only an extension of the

Deutsche mark. Giddy from the political success of reunification, in spite of its astronomical costs, they are victims of their new international ambition and a bulimia of power after a half-century of diplomatic frustration, and can only be flattered by the prospect of leading a nation of 280 million inhabitants.

But the leading role in this affair belongs to France. Our elites are indeed incapable of conceiving of a continental society not governed by a central State, whereas Germany has a federal and decentralized constitution. It is also France that had been blindly pursuing, since the inter-war period, the Holy Grail of fixed exchange rates. The Bundesbank does not consider the parity of the mark as an objective of monetary policy, which means quite simply that Germany adopts, for all practical purposes, a policy of floating exchange rates. And finally, it is the will for power of our unanimous politico-administrative class, which reconciles Gaullism and socialism in the continuation of the old dream of controlling Germanic economic power in the service of its own grandeur, which constitutes the deep wellspring of this noxious enterprise.

This policy, counter to the national interests, testifies, in the two countries, to a growing divergence between leaders and voters. The construction of the single currency and the super-State corresponds to the interests of the former. It results in a double rejection of the market mechanism: the refusal to allow the free play of exchange markets (whereas everywhere else in the world the trend is, since the abandonment of the system of Bretton Woods, for the adoption of floating rates), and also the rejection of competition between State-enterprises in the European free trade zone. Instead of allowing the "national enterprises," which are the States, to compete among themselves to attract companies and capital, the formation of a single State would replace the competitive play of nations with a decision-making process within only one bureaucracy, vertically integrated.

That naturally corresponds to the preferences of the civil servants and politicians: to maximize the number of positions and to maximize their power over the rest of society. The growth of the hierarchical pyramids enables them to be freed more comfortably from the taxpayers' and the consumers' control.

It is the constant tendency of hierarchies, the technostructure—in a word, bureaucracy—gradually to establish its autonomy from those whose interests it administers and who are supposed, in a democracy, to control it and use it to their own ends. The weakening of democracy allows for this drift, which corporate economists would qualify as "managerial deviation." It is accompanied by collusion between the controllers and the controlled, within a single politico-administrative caste that functions in a closed loop and independently of the expectations of the public.

However, in putting itself beyond the real control of the voters, the leading class loses access to information pertaining to developments within the country and then persists in the unremitting pursuit of its narrow interests, which may constitute as many costly errors.

The process is quite similar to that of managerial independence of companies that escape their shareholders, who are dispossessed of their power in favor of the managers. The managers consequently become insensitive to the preferences of their principals and can give way with impunity to the heady will for power, constantly enlarging the scope of their authority, even if this results in a reduction in the value of the enterprise.

In the case of the euro, the enterprise is the State, but its value is just as easily ruined by managerialism as that of any private company[1]. Indeed, in any hierarchical organization, be it of a commercial enterprise or the State, the separation of control and decision-making is essential to good management. The last word belongs with those who pay, whether the shareholders or the taxpayers, if one wants to obtain the most effective use of the available resources and to enrich the community.

Such is the role of the shareholding, the takeover offers and the financial markets on one side, and real and competitive democracy on the other. But when management ends up as one with the board of directors, when the civil servants and politicians together unite in one quasi-autonomous class, the base loses any real control. Then shareholders, customers, taxpayers have no more hope of making their votes heard.

This is why the pursuit of the plan for a single currency and single State constitutes a good prospect for the politico-administrative apparatus, but a worrying adventure for the well being of the Frenchmen, in particular, and Europeans in general.

What can be done to avoid the disaster? In the presence of a pernicious plan the only reasonable response is to give it up. An about-face must be made. In fact, we must turn our back on the single currency and refuse to build a single State in Europe. But it will not be easy. Not because abandoning the euro would expose us to some economic catastrophe, a threat that the fundamentalists brandish, just as they threatened all the worst yesterday if England gave up its fixed parity with the mark. What succeeded so well in Great Britain will also succeed with France and the other European countries. Abandoning the single currency will enable them to find the way to prosperity.

The difficulty, actually, will consist in giving up a plan that is so much in accord with the ideas and the interests of the politico-administrative class. Turning our back on the single currency and the single State equates to a democratic questioning of French technocracy, that is, of the French exception in a world which grants more and more scope to market mechanisms and political democracy. Our leading class understands this very well, and turns it into a dogma in support of its conservative bent. It does not intend to accept the erosion of its discretionary powers.

However, there is a solution to stagnation in Europe. It is known, and its effectiveness is not in doubt. It is within reach and can quickly be put in place. But our political leaders do not want to hear talk of this. Prisoners of false conceptions and chimerical objectives, as in the Thirties, they will yield probably only at the last moment, when faced with the ruin of the economy and the democratic revolt of the populace.

Just as the voters, in earlier times, forced the abandonment of financial conservatism and of the gold standard in favor of a policy of reflation, floating currencies and a return to full employment, at the end of this century they are moving toward a systematic rejection, by successive majorities, of those who refuse to listen to reason and persist in establishing relative deflation, overvaluation of the currency, and further development of an already hypertrophied political superstructure.

To give up the single currency and the single State would constitute, in sum, a democratic revolution in our republican monarchy. There is just time enough to get ready, while waiting for the euro to fail, which is sure to upset profoundly the traditional political balances.

NOTES

Introduction

1. *The European Miracle,* Environments, Economics and Geopolitics in the History of Europe and Asia, Cambridge University Press, 1981.

Chapter I

1. "Crime and Punishment: An Economic Approach," *Journal of Political Economy,* March-April 1968.
2. *Autopsie d'une émeute. Histoire exemplaire du soulèvement d'un quartier,* Albin Michel, 1997.
3. According to a study by Jeff Grogger, "Market Wages and Youth Crime," *NBER Working Paper* No. 5983, March 1997.
4. *Perspectives de l'emploi,* 1993.
5. See for example my article "Le smic, un destructeur d'emploi," *Le Monde des Débats,* September 1994.
6. In *Le Rapport Rosa* (Volume 1, *La Macro-économie et l'Etat,* Bonnel, 1983).
7. This is particularly so in the case of the study by Nicholas F.R. Crafts and Terence C. Mills, "Europe's Golden Age: An Econometric Investigation of Changing Trend Rates of Growth," *CEPR* No. 1087, January 1995.
8. This is illustrated particularly clearly in a study by Angel de la Fuente ("Catch-up, Growth and Convergence in the OECD," *CEPR Working Paper* No. 1274, November 1995) on the convergence of the levels of technology and their links to research and development costs.
9. Variations in social security spending expressed as a percentage of the GDP and variations in the rate of unemployment

247

Country	Variations in social spending % of GNP 1960/1988	Variations in unemployment tax 1969/1973-1986/1992
Spain	4.30	15.4
Denmark	2.64	9.8
France	2.40	7.3
Belgium	2.25	6.5
Italy	2.18	4.8
Great Britain	2.03	5.6
Germany	1.46	4.6
Ireland	1.20	9.8

* Social security spending includes illness, infirmity, old age, unemployment, family allowances, maternity allowances, vocational training and housing allowances.

Source: Meltzer A. H., "Commentary," in *Reducing Unemployment: Current Exits and Policy Options,* Federal Reserve Bank of Kansas City, 1994.

10. "Past and Prospective Causes of High Unemployment," *Reducing Unemployment: Current Issues and Policy Options,* Federal Reserve Bank of Kansas City, 1994.
11. "Sense and Nonsense in the Globalization Debate," *Foreign Policy,* Summer 1997, as well as his work *Has Globalization Gone Too Far?,* Institute for International Economics, 1997.
12. In particular Robert Barro in his recent study, *Determinants of Economic Growth, A Cross-Country Empirical Study,* MIT Press, 1997, and Robert E. Hall and Charles I. Jones in their article "The Productivity of Nations," *NBER Working Paper,* November 1996.
13. Barry Eichengreen, *Golden Fetters: The Gold Standard and the Great Depression, 1919-1939,* Oxford University Press, 1995.
14. As shown by Robert J. Gordon ("Macroeconomic Policy in the Presence of Structural Maladjustment," *NBER Working Paper* No. 5739, September 1996) and Alberto Alesina and Roberto Perotti ("Fiscal Expansions and Fiscal Adjustment in OECD Countries," NBER *Working Paper* No. 5214, August 1995).
15. As Robert Barro attempts to show, in *Getting it Right, Markets and Choices in a Free Society* , Ch. 2, MIT Press, 1996.
16. He proposes a brilliant analysis of this in his article "Contre l'intégrisme monétaire," *Politique Internationale,* Winter 1996-1997.
17. This is strongly emphasized by Barry Eichengreen and Marc Uzan, "The 1933 World Economic Conference as an Instance of Failed International Cooperation," in Peter B. Evans and Al, eds., *Double-Edged Diplomacy,* University of California Press, 1993.

Chapter II

1. This theory was developed simultaneously by Milton Friedman ("The Role of Monetary Policy," *American Economic Review,* March 1968) and Edmund Phelps ("Money-Wage Dynamics and Labor Market Equilibrium," *Journal of Political*

Economy, 1968).

2. "The Relation between Unemployment and the Rate of Change of Money-Wage Rates in the United Kingdom, 1861-1957," *Economica,* November 1958.

3. "A Sticky-Price Manifesto," *NBER Working Paper* No. 4677, March 1994.

4. "Does Monetary Policy Matter? At New Test in the Spirit of Friedman and Schwartz," *NBER Macroeconomics Annual,* 1989.

5. "What Determines the Sacrifice Ratio?" *NBER Working Paper* No. 4306, 1993.

6. "The Time-Varying NAIRU and its Implications for Economic Policy," *NBER Working Paper,* No. 5735, August 1996.

7. This is particularly the case of the Harvard economist Gregory Mankiw in his article "Small Menu Costs and Broad Business Cycles: A Macroeconomic Model of Monopoly ," *Quarterly Newspaper of Economics,* 1985.

8. As Laurence Ball and Gregory Mankiw show in "Relative-Price Price Changes as Aggregate Supply Shocks," *Quarterly Journal of Economics,* February 1995.

9. Geoffrey M.B. Tootell, "Central Bank Flexibility and the Drawback to Currency Unification," *New England Economic Review,* May-June 1990.

10. Atish R. Gosh and Holger C. Wolf, "How Many Monies? A Genetic Approach to Finding Optimum Currency Areas," *NBER Working Paper* No. 4805, July 1994.

11. "The Case against EMU," *The Economist,* June 13, 1992.

12. "Fiscal Federalism and Optimum Currency Areas: Evidence for Europe from the United States," *NBER, Working Paper,* October 1991.

13. "Exchange Rates and Economic Recovery in the 1930s, *The Journal of Economic History,* December 1985.

14. "Macroeconomic Policy in the Presence of Structural Maladjustment," *NBER Working Paper* No. 5739, September 1996.

15. Edmund Phelps, "Le chômage structurel: causes et remèdes," *Le Figaro,* May 27, 1994.

16. As Allechi M'Bet and Amlan Madeleine Niamkey show, "European Economic Integration and the Franc Zone: The future of the CFA Franc after 1996," *African Economic Research Consortium,* July 1993.

17. *Bulletin of the IMF,* March 14, 1994.

18. This is the approach taken by, for example, Jürgen von Hagen and Manfred J. M. Neumann ("Real Exchange Rates Within and Between Currency Areas: How Far Away is EMU?," *The Review of Economics and Statistics,* 1994) as well as Tamim Bayoumi and Barry Eichengreen ("One Money or Many? Analyzing the Prospects for Monetary Unification in Various Parts of the World," *Princeton Studies in International Finance,* September 1994).

19. See below, p. 302.

20. The optimal exchange regime —Heller Method

Year	Country interested to protect floating exchanges			Country interested to enter in a Deutsche mark area			
	Germany	France	Italy	U K	Belgium	Denmark	Netherlands
1975	5.47	4.28	2.74	3.98	-1.78	-1.53	-0.86
1980	6.68	5.24	3.85	4.30	-1.57	-1.50	-0.74
1985	7.14	5.82	4.31	5.26	-1.72	-1.42	-0.77
1990	8.79	7.11	5.39	6.26	-1.48	-1.21	-0.32

Statistical sources: OECD, IMF

19. Particularly Robert Heller ("Determinants of Exchange Rates Practices," *Journal of Money, Credit and Banking,* August 1978), Paul Holden, Merle Holden and Esther C. Suss ("The Determinants of Exchange Rate Flexibility: An Empirical Investigation," *The Review of Economics and Statistics,* August 1979) and Gordon Weil (*Exchange-Rate Regime Selection in Theory and in Practice,* Salomon Brothers Center for the Study of Financial Institutions, 1983).
20. See above, p. 301.
21. A slightly different calculation, following Gordon Weil's method again which relies on the characteristics of economic openness, relative inflation, geographical diversification of foreign trade, and mobility of resources, leads to a similar conclusion. The Weil index lies between zero and one. Proximity to zero leads to fluctuating exchanges, proximity to one leads to fixed rates. One may consider the dividing line therefore to be at a value of 0.5 on the index. Above that, the country has an interest to implement a fixed exchange regime, below that, to implement flexible exchanges. Applying this index to the various European countries shows once again that France, Germany and the United Kingdom have characteristics which call for floating exchanges, while Italy, Belgium and the Netherlands are find themselves more on the side of fixed exchanges.

The regime of optimal flexibility — Gordon Weil's Method

Year	Y * France	Y U K	Y Germany	Y Italy	Y Denmark	Y Netherlands	Y Belgium
1975	0.1805	0.2206	0.2023	0.2569	0.2614	0.2668	0.2915
1980	0.1938	0.1299	0.22386	0.1959	0.2736	0.3377	0.3236
1985	0.1905	0.1080	0.2430	0.1973	0.2575	0.4053	0.3398
1990	0.1960	0.1944	0.2449	0.2076	0.2466	0.2450	0.3259

* Y is the probability of being in fixed exchanges such that $0<Y<1$.

Statistical sources: OECD, IMF.

22. Ben S. Bernanke, "The Macroeconomics of the Great Depression: A Comparative Approach," *Journal of Money, Credit and Banking,* February 1995, page 4.
23. In *Courrier international* (July 24-30, 1997).
24. *European Monetary Union since 1848: A Political and Historical Analysis,* Edward Elgar, 1996.

Chapter III

1. *Determinants of Economic Growth, A Cross-Country Empirical Study,* MIT Press, 1997.
2. "The Productivity of Nations," *NBER Working Paper* No. 5812, November 1996.
3. "The Growth Tax in the United States," *Public Choice,* 1995.
4. "The Optimal Government Size: Further International Evidence on the Productivity of Government Services," *Economic Inquiry,* April 1996.
5. As Michael Piore and Charles Sabel demonstrate in their book *The Second Industrial Divide,* Basic Books, 1984.
6. Mimeographed document, MIT, 1979.
7. "Employment in Small and Large Firms: Where Have the Jobs Come From?," *Employment Outlook,* September 1985.

8. "The Re-emergence of Small-Scale Production: An International Comparison," *Small Business Economics*, No. 3, pp. 1-37, 1991.
9. As Rexford E. Santerre and Stephen P. Neun show, in "Corporate Control and Performance in the 1930s," *Economic Inquiry*, July 1993.
10. According to a revealing study by Constantinos C. Markides, *Diversification, Refocusing, and Economic Performance*, MIT Press, 1995.
11. "The Use of Knowledge in Society," *American Economic Review*, September 1945.
12. Angus Maddison, *L'Economie mondiale 1820-1992, Analyse et statistiques*, OECD, 1995.
13. *The Word and the Sword, How Techniques of Information and Violence Have Shaped Our World*, Blackwell, 1991, pp. 272-275.
14. Friday, April 4, 1997.
15. *Power, Trade, and War*, Princeton University Press, 1994.
16. Albin Michel, 1996.
17. Jeffrey Frankel, Ernesto Stein, Shang-jin Wei, "Continental Trading Blocks: Are they Super-Natural or Natural?," *NBER Working Paper* No. 4588, December 1993.
18. *Parkinson's Law and Other Studies in Administration*, Ballantine, 1957.
19. *Markets and Hierarchies: Analysis and Antitrust Implications*, Free Press, 1975.
20. "The Nature of the Firm," *Economica*, 1937.
21. See Julian Franks and Colin Mayer, "Corporate Ownership and Control in the U.K., Germany, and France," *Journal of Applied Corporate Finance*, Winter 1997.
22. Rafael La Porta, Florencio Lopez-de-Silanes, Andrei Shleifer, Robert W Vishny, "Legal Determinants of External Finance," *NBER Working Paper* No. 5879, January 1997.
23. As shown by Armen Alchian and Harold Demsetz, who are at the forefront of contemporary theory on companies and organizations ("Production, Information Costs, and Economic Organization," *American Economic Review*, 1972).
24. This is what Albert Breton and Ronald Wintrobe stress in their work, *The Logic of Bureaucratic Conduct. An Analysis of Competition, Exchange and Efficiency in Private and Public Organizations*, Cambridge University Press, 1982.
25. "Europe's Dash for the Future," August 13, 1994.
26. See in particular my articles "De l'inculture économique," an interview published in *Le Figaro*, July 17, 1981, and "L'économie globale et les désarrois devant le marché," *Le Figaro*, December 20, 1991.
27. *La Construction de l'Etat moderne en Europe*, University Presses of France, 1994.
28. In a book on the *Ressorts cachés de la réussite française*, Seuil, 1995.
29. In particular in *Les Elites en France, Grands corps et grandes écoles*, Seuil, 1979.
30. *La Noblesse d'Etat. Grandes écoles et esprit de corps*, Editions de Minuit, 1989.
31. Which Elie Cohen grippingly illustrates in *L'Etat brancardier : politique du déclin industriel, 1974-1984*, Calmann-Lévy, 1989.
32. It is the group of "New Economists" whom I convened with Florin Aftalion to publish *L'Economique retrouvée*, Economica, 1978.
33. *The World Crisis in Social Security*, Bonnel, 1982.
34. "The Modern Industrial Revolution, Exit, and the Failure of Internal Control Systems," *Journal of Applied Corporate Finance*, Winter 1994.
35. *International Herald Tribune*, June 14-15, 1997.

Chapter IV

1. "Fiscal Adjustment in OECD Countries: Composition and Macroeconomic Effects,"
    NBER Working Paper No. 5730, August 1996.
2. *Redresser l'économie de la France,* Economica, 1997.

Conclusion

1. As I show in my article on "La valeur de l'Etat," *Le Figaro,* January 26, 1995.

Also from Algora Publishing:

CLAUDIU A. SECARA
THE NEW COMMONWEALTH
From Bureaucratic Corporatism to Socialist Capitalism

The notion of an elite-driven worldwide perestroika has gained some credibility lately. The book examines in a historical perspective the most intriguing dialectic in the Soviet Union's "collapse" — from socialism to capitalism and back to socialist capitalism — and speculates on the global implications.

IGNACIO RAMONET
THE GEOPOLITICS OF CHAOS

The author, Director of *Le Monde Diplomatique*, presents an original, discriminating and lucid political matrix for understanding what he calls the "current disorder of the world" in terms of Internationalization, Cyberculture and Political Chaos.

TZVETAN TODOROV
A PASSION FOR DEMOCRACY –
Benjamin Constant

The French Revolution rang the death knell not only for a form of society, but also for a way of feeling and of living; and it is still not clear as yet what did we gain from the changes.

MICHEL PINÇON & MONIQUE PINÇON-CHARLOT
GRAND FORTUNES
Dynasties of Wealth in France

Going back for generations, the fortunes of great families consist of far more than money—they are also symbols of culture and social interaction. They are at the heart of dense family and extra-family networks, of international coalitions and divisions. The authors elucidate the machinery of accumulation and the paradoxically quasi-collective nature of private fortunes.

CLAUDIU A. SECARA
TIME & EGO
Judeo-Christian Egotheism and the Anglo-Saxon Industrial Revolution

The first question of abstract reflection that arouses controversy is the problem of Becoming. Being persists, beings constantly change; they are born and they pass away. How can Being change and yet be eternal? The quest for the logical and experimental answer has just taken off.

JEAN-MARIE ABGRALL
SOUL SNATCHERS: THE MECHANICS OF CULTS

Jean-Marie Abgrall, psychiatrist, criminologist, expert witness to the French Court of Appeals, and member of the Inter-Ministry Committee on Cults, is one of the experts most frequently consulted by the European judicial and legislative processes. The fruit of fifteen years of research, his book delivers the first methodical analysis of the sectarian phenomenon, decoding the mental manipulation on behalf of mystified observers as well as victims.

JEAN-CLAUDE GUILLEBAUD
THE TYRANNY OF PLEASURE

The ambition of the book is to pose clearly and without subterfuge the question of sexual morals -- that is, the place of the forbidden -- in a modern society. For almost a whole generation, we have lived in the illusion that this question had ceased to exist. Today the illusion is faded, but a strange and tumultuous distress replaces it. No longer knowing very clearly where we stand, our societies painfully seek answers between unacceptable alternatives: bold-faced permissiveness or nostalgic moralism.

SOPHIE COIGNARD AND MARIE-THÉRÈSE GUICHARD
FRENCH CONNECTIONS
The Secret History of Networks of Influence

They were born in the same region, went to the same schools, fought the same fights and made the same mistakes in youth. They share the same morals, the same fantasies of success and the same taste for money. They act behind the scenes to help each other, boosting careers, monopolizing business and information, making money, conspiring and, why not, becoming Presidents!

VLADIMIR PLOUGIN
INTELLIGENCE HAS ALWAYS EXISTED

This collection contains the latest works by historians, investigating the most mysterious episodes from Russia's past. All essays are based on thorough studies of preserved documents. The book discusses the establishment of secret services in Kievan Rus, and describes heroes and systems of intelligence and counterintelligence in the 16th-17th centuries. Semen Maltsev, a diplomat of Ivan the Terrible's times is presented as well as the much publicised story of the abduction of "Princess Tarakanova".